Wicked,
Wicked Libels

Wicked, Wicked Libels

edited by

Michael Rubinstein

Routledge & Kegan Paul

London and Boston

First published 1972
by Routledge & Kegan Paul Ltd
Broadway House, 68–74 Carter Lane
London EC4V 5EL and
9 Park Street
Boston, Mass. 02108, U.S.A.
Printed in Great Britain by
The Camelot Press Ltd
London and Southampton

ISBN 0 7100 7239 2

Contents

Acknowledgments

The editor and publishers would like to thank the following for permission to reproduce copyright material:

Mrs Frida Laski and the *Atlantic Monthly* for 'My Day in Court', by Harold Laski. Copyright 1952, by The Atlantic Monthly Company, Boston, Mass. Reprinted with permission.

The *Financial Times* for 'Punitive Damages and the PQ 17 Libel Case', by 'Justinian'.

Contributors

Louis Abraham was an authority on parliamentary law until his retirement.

Louis Blom-Cooper, Q.C. is an author and maverick lawyer who has shown interest in the problems of censorship and privacy.

Eugene Gros has worked as a design engineer, author, technical journalist, translator and as consultant on information processing to the U.S. Library of Congress. At present he is Managing Director of a company specializing in processing and publishing scientific and technical information.

H. Montgomery Hyde, author and barrister, has written widely in the areas of literature and the law.

Richard Ingrams has been Editor of *Private Eye* since 1963.

William ('Peter') Kimber is Managing Director of William Kimber & Co. Ltd, who were defendant publishers in one of the most notable libel cases ever to be tried in the High Court, brought by the doctor from Auschwitz. He is a member of the Libel Committee of the Publishers' Association and a member of the Lord Chancellor's Committee on Defamation.

Cecil H. King was formerly Chairman of Daily Mirror Newspapers Ltd and Sunday Pictorial Newspapers Ltd.

Anthony Lincoln, Q.C., who is a member of the Common Law Bar, is a writer and broadcaster on legal and press affairs.

Michael Rubinstein is a solicitor specializing in literary legal matters. He is no less interested in social, psychological and philosophical knowledge and the subtle influences that motivate human thinking and behaviour in society today. He is a member of the Lord Chancellor's Committee on Defamation.

Introduction

The Popular Appetite for Scandal

Michael Rubinstein

'Nothing to excess.' So, truth will out – but not too much of it. As for the rest (all vanity?), that is presumably lies, all lies: let us not have too much of them either. The complex web of living extends from the nucleus of fact through statistics, opinions and fancies to the perimeter of illusion – and back to the nucleus with healthy disillusionment: life would be dull without this variety. Indeed life would be dull without at least occasional excesses – within limits.

This book is about excesses and limits in the realm of communication. We communicate with each other through our personalities yet at the same time it is our personalities which insulate us from each other. Hence real or imagined damage to our personalities at the same time seems to threaten both the nature and quality of our relationships, indeed our very ability to relate to others, and our psychological armour, our 'dignity'.

> Dignity is expected particularly of people in positions of authority, and that is why the insinuation of obscene or undignified behaviour among public figures is a potent weapon of satire. The popular appetite for scandal in high places is an indication of pleasure at seeing the dignified* brought down to a less respectable status. Because of the intimate connection between dignity and authority . . . protecting dignity by censorship in effect bolsters up the order of authority.[1]

* . . . man, proud man,
Drest in a little brief authority.

The law of libel is the instrument of censorship by which dignity – too often pseudo-dignity – is to be upheld. Like the law of the land throughout its whole range, it is but a blunt instrument; it metes out that mean measure of justice which is the most that imperfect man can offer to imperfect man.

Satire and scandal are colourful. Justice is not after all blind, only colour-blind; it assesses the balance of grey between off-white and off-black. The law is the blunt instrument of pragmatism, only a coarse replica of the sword of enlightenment wielded by an angel of the Lord and brandished so successfully in the often cited judgment of Solomon K.[2]

Man-made justice is a relative thing, inevitably. English law lacks even a relatively absolute 'Code Wellington' or anything like that; traditionally it is said to evolve by precedent – much as the motor car or any other machine can be said to evolve, by discrete degrees. Of our man-made law it can be said '*Le Loi est mort – Vive le Loi!*' As we do not have absolute law so there can be no absolute record of our law: in relation to libel, *Gatley* may be the 'bible' but it is not *The Bible*.

Still less is this little collection of essays, some by lawyers and others by laymen, a well-illuminated comprehensive commentary; it is rather a battery of spotlights, in places overlapping. May it entertain as well as enlighten!

M. B. R.

References

1 Mr Alan Segal of Goldsmiths' College quoted in Science Report, *The Times*, 20 April 1970, extracted from *British Journal of Sociology*, 1970, 21, 63.
2 I Kgs. 3:28.

One

A Look at the Law

H. Montgomery Hyde

I

'Hold your tongue!' is a species of advice not always followed by those who publish or utter imputations defamatory of the characters of others. If it were, criminal prosecutions for libel and civil actions for libel or slander would never be brought in the courts. Unfortunately there is no wholly satisfactory definition of a defamatory imputation. The classical definition in English law was given by a judge in the middle of the nineteenth century[1] as

> a publication without justification or lawful excuse which is calculated to injure the reputation of another by exposing him to hatred, contempt or ridicule.

This definition has been criticized as being too narrow. For instance, certain suggestions which might be very injurious to the reputation of a business man, such as insolvency not due to any disreputable conduct on his part, would not be covered by it. In the Report of the Select Committee of the House of Lords appointed in 1843 to consider the law of defamation, the Lord Chancellor Lord Lyndhurst said that he 'had never yet seen or been able to hit upon anything like a definition of libel which possessed the requisites of a logical definition'. However, his judicial colleague Lord Campbell, who was to introduce in the same year the parliamentary Act amending the law of libel which bears his name, did attempt one, namely,

> a writing tending to injure or degrade the character of the person who is the object of it.

If the expression 'writing' is extended to include any form of permanent matter such as statues, waxworks, drawings, photographs, cartoons, radio broadcasts, and motion pictures whether cinema or television, then Lord Campbell's definition is probably about as good a definition of libel as we are ever likely to get.

The incautious author of a libel or slander may well live to regret his (or her) action, when eventually saddled with a large bill for damages and costs. On the other hand, anyone thinking of issuing a writ for defamation of character is often well advised to hold his horses. If he does not go into the witness-box and tell his story in his own words, he may get little sympathy from the jury. On the other hand, if he does give evidence, he is liable to be cross-examined as to his conduct and character, and in the result may sustain infinitely more injury than he has already sustained from the actual defamatory words. There is an old case which was recalled by Chief Justice Holt when sitting on the judicial bench in the reign of Queen Anne, where the plaintiff brought an action for slander against a man who had said he was 'a highwayman'. The defendant pleaded justification – that is, he undertook to prove the truth of his allegation. He did so to the satisfaction of the jury. The result was that, besides losing his action, the plaintiff was arrested before he left the court, was duly convicted of being a highwayman, committed to Newgate gaol and hanged. Hence, in Chief Justice Holt's words, 'people ought to advise well before they bring such actions'.[2] Similarly in 1895, when Oscar Wilde unwisely prosecuted Lord Queensberry for criminal libel – Queensberry had described Wilde as 'posing as a sodomite' – the defendant successfully pleaded justification. Wilde was arrested later the same day on homosexual charges and eventually went to prison for two years.[3] Also the facts elicited in cross-examination may result in a verdict for contemptuous damages and an order depriving the successful plaintiff of his or her costs. In the action brought by the artist James McNeill Whistler against the art critic John Ruskin, this directly led to the plaintiff's bankruptcy.

In English law there are differences in substance and procedure between the two kinds of defamation – libel (written or printed) and slander (spoken). These differences, which do not exist in other legal codes and systems, are the result of historical accident. Briefly, they stem from the fact that libel was originally regarded as a crime regardless of its truth or falsity, and punishable by the King's courts, while slander, unless uttered about the sovereign or officials of the government, was treated as a private wrong primarily within the jurisdiction of the ecclesiastical courts, a jurisdiction which, though it became virtually obsolete by the beginning of the last century, was not formally abolished until 1855. Also slander was not generally actionable except on proof of 'special damage', i.e. actual pecuniary loss, whereas libel proceedings could be brought on proof of publication only, the difference supposedly depending upon the permanent form of libel as contrasted with the relative impermanence of slander.

At common law there were certain specific slanderous accusations which were always actionable without proof of special damage – specifically the imputation of a punishable crime or a disease and the disparagement of a person in his office, profession or business. To these were added a significant statutory exception. When the jurisdiction of the ecclesiastical courts was abolished, women were left at a disadvantage in that they had to prove monetary loss as the result of an accusation of moral incontinence. The Church courts, of course, did not demand proof of special damage in such cases, since incontinence was regarded by these courts as a sin and punishable by penance and fine. But the civil courts did and such proof was extremely difficult and often impossible to obtain. Consequently in 1891 Parliament passed the Slander of Women Act, which dispensed with the requirement of proving special damage where the words complained of imputed adultery or unchastity to a woman or girl. In a comparatively recent case, a statement made by one woman about another that 'she used to live with other women – she is a Lesbian' was held to be an imputation of unchastity within the meaning of the statute, and therefore it was not necessary for the plaintiff to prove actual pecuniary damage.[4]

As might be expected, before the discovery of printing, most of the early actions for defamation were for slander. The first reported case occurred in 1356 when a woman named Lucy was alleged to have called Mr Justice Seton, judge of the Court of Exchequer, a 'traitor, felon and robber'. The judge sued Lucy for slander claiming £1,000 damages, but the jury reduced this figure to 100 marks (£33 6s. 8d.).

The appearance of the printing press brought libel into prominence, and for long this was regarded as exclusively a criminal offence, due no doubt to the fact that all publications had to be licensed by the government and consequently proceedings for libel were usually brought in respect of unauthorized publications. Many such cases were tried by the notorious Court of Star Chamber in the early part of the seventeenth century, and that court gradually adopted the practice of awarding damages to the party injured by the libel as well as punishment for the crime of publication. This in turn led to the growth of the idea that libel might also be treated as a civil wrong or tort. Civil actions for libel may in general be said to date from the abolition of the Star Chamber court in 1641, but at first they were infrequently brought as compared with prosecutions for criminal libel. The criminal origin of libel survives today in civil actions, where to succeed it is not necessary for the plantiff to prove actual damage, as distinct from slander where it usually is.

Until towards the end of the eighteenth century the only question which judges were in the habit of leaving for the consideration of the jury in libel proceedings was that of publication – that is, whether the defendant had actually published the words complained of. Then in 1792, after much agitation, Parliament passed the celebrated Act associated with the Whig statesman Charles James Fox, usually known as Fox's Libel Act. This measure, originally applied to criminal proceedings but subsequently extended by analogy to civil actions for libel, gave the jury the definite power to find a general verdict of Guilty or Not Guilty – in other words, libel or no libel, provided always that the publication complained of is capable of a defamatory meaning. As a nineteenth-century judge put it, 'if a publication, either standing alone, or taken in connection with other circumstances, is reasonably capable of a libellous construction, it is for the jury, and not for the court, to say whether a libellous construction should be put upon it.'[5]

The question of whether or not the words complained of are capable of conveying a defamatory meaning, and consequently whether they should be left to the jury, can sometimes be an extremely difficult one. For if the judge errs in this respect, the decision will be upset by a higher court on appeal. The leading case on the question is *Capital & Counties Bank* v. *Henty*, which was decided in the eighties of the last century. The facts were simple enough, but whether in the circumstances the words complained of were or were not libellous was a matter which taxed the greatest judicial brains of the day.

Henty's were a firm of brewers in Chichester, and they owned a considerable number of inns in Sussex and Hampshire, to which they supplied their own brew of beer. They allowed their accounts with these inns to be settled from time to time with cheques drawn on the Capital & Counties Bank, and they used to pay the cheques into the Chichester branch of the bank for which they received cash. In 1878 a new manager arrived at this branch and refused to cash cheques drawn on other branches of the bank by persons unknown to him. This was a particularly unfortunate decision, since the first cheque to be refused was only for £5 and only two other cheques for a total of £42 had been presented during the year. The manager remained adamant, and in consequence Henty's sent out the following printed notice to their tenants and customers, 137 in all, in the various public houses:

> Messrs Henty & Sons hereby give notice that they will no longer receive in payment cheques drawn on any of the branches of the Capital and Counties Bank.

This circular notice became known to others, and in the result there was a run on the bank amounting to £277,000. The bank thereupon brought an action for libel against Henty's on the ground that the circular in its effect implied that the bank was insolvent or was on the verge of insolvency. In their defence Henty's denied that the notice had any such meaning, and pleaded that in the circumstances they had a lawful interest in communicating it to their customers, and that they were not liable unless malice could be proved against them.

The case was tried by Lord Chief Justice Coleridge and a special jury.* It was argued strongly for the plaintiff bank

* Special juries were drawn from the better-to-do members of the community with a property qualification, and unlike common juries were paid for their services. They were abolished in 1949.

that a defamatory interpretation had been put upon the notice by many of their customers. The defendants, on the other hand, argued that there were other interpretations, and anyhow they had only done something which they were perfectly entitled to do – that is, to refuse to accept the cheques of a particular bank – and there was no other way in which they could have expressed their refusal except by written notice. To this the bank rejoined that the majority of the defendant's customers were ignorant of the dispute between Henty's and the bank and the notice should have contained some indication of it. Whatever Henty's intentions were, there was no doubt that the bank had suffered grievous loss by reason of the notice. In the event the trial judge ruled that the notice was capable of a defamatory meaning and left the question to the jury. However, the jury could not agree on a verdict and had to be discharged. Naturally the bank wanted a new trial, but it was argued for Henty's before two judges in a divisional court that the words were not capable of a defamatory meaning and therefore there was nothing for a jury to decide, and so the defendants were entitled to judgment. The judges sided with Lord Coleridge, and the matter went to the Court of Appeal, which overruled the divisional court by a majority of two to one. This decision was in turn upheld by the House of Lords by a majority of four to one, which meant that the notice was not defamatory, and the bank lost its case. In all six judges supported this finding, while five were against it.

The majority in the supreme appellate court approved the dictum of Lord Justice Brett, later Lord Esher, Master of the Rolls, in the Court of Appeal, as a useful yardstick in approaching the question of libel or no libel, and one which is still applied. 'It is unreasonable that, where there are a number of good interpretations, the only bad one should be seized upon to give a defamatory sense to the document.' That is a common-sense view, but it took eleven judges in seventy closely printed pages of judicial reasoning to arrive at it.[6]

II

The two great legislative milestones in the history of the English law of defamation, apart from Fox's Libel Act already mentioned, were both the result of recommendations of parliamentary committees. The first of these milestones was the Libel Act, 1843, commonly called Lord Campbell's Act, which resulted from the Report of a Select Committee of the House of Lords. On the criminal side the Act provided that it should be a good defence to plead the truth of the alleged libel, provided also that 'it was for the public benefit that the said matters charged should be published'. Hitherto a plea of justification was unacceptable in a prosecution for criminal libel, it being commonly said that 'the greater the truth, the greater the libel'. The truth of the matter complained of had always been a good defence in civil actions for libel or slander, and the House of Lords Select Committee recommended that proof of public benefit should also be required in all defamation proceedings whether criminal or civil. However, the Act as eventually passed by Parliament restricted this proposed additional requirement to defences in criminal prosecutions only. On the other hand, the Act contained an important amendment to the civil law affecting newspapers, which for the first time enabled a newspaper to set up the defence that the libel was inserted in the newspaper without actual malice and without gross negligence, and furthermore that the defendant newspaper had published an apology and paid a sum by way of damages into court.

The only other official committee to consider the English law of defamation was appointed in 1939 and is generally known as the Porter Committee from the name of the able lawyer, Lord Porter, who was its chairman. Its deliberations were interrupted by the war, and it was not able to report until 1948. Four years more were to elapse before any of its recommendations were adopted. The Defamation Act 1952 provided that defamatory matter broadcast over the radio should be treated as libel and not slander, thus making it actionable without proof of special damage; also, that in cases of unintentional defamation a person who claims that he or she published the alleged defamatory words 'innocently' in relation to the person defamed may escape liability for damages, if certain conditions are fulfilled as to the defendant's intention, state of knowledge and care shown over publication.*

* The publisher must prove:
1 (a) that he did not intend to publish the alleged defamatory

The Porter Committee received evidence from a number of representative authors, publishers and printers on the subject of unintentional defamation, and these witnesses suggested that the type of defamatory statement in respect of which protection from liability for damages was most needed fell into two classes:

(1) Statements not *intended* to refer to the plaintiff at all, e.g.
  (a) statements intended to refer to a fictitious character, but in fact defamatory of an existing person; or
  (b) statements truthfully made of an existing person but in fact defamatory of another existing person.
(2) Statements intended to refer to an existing person, which although on their face harmless are, by reason of facts unknown to the author or publisher, defamatory either of the person intended to be referred to, or of some other person.

In particular, the Committee was reminded of three decided cases, which they felt called for a change in the law. (See Report of the Porter Committee, para. 60.)

The first of these cases concerned a person who was intended to be a fictitious character but who turned out to be a real person. In July 1908 the Paris correspondent of the *Sunday Chronicle* was asked to write an article about Dieppe and its Motor Week. He did so and for the purpose of enlivening the article which he entitled 'Motor-Mad Dieppe' he introduced a fictitious character whom he called 'Artemus Jones'. The following is an extract from this article:

> Upon the terrace marches the world, attracted by the motor races – a world immensely pleased with itself, and minded to draw a wealth of inspiration – and, incidentally, of golden cocktails – from any scheme to speed the passing hour . . .

---

words and was unaware of the circumstances by virtue of which they might be understood to refer to the complainant; or

(b) that the words were not defamatory on the face of them, and that he was unaware of the foregoing circumstances; and

2 in either event, that he exercised reasonable care in relation to the publication.

> Whist! There is Artemus Jones with a woman who is not his wife, who must be, you know – the other thing! whispers a fair neighbour of mine excitedly into her bosom friend's ear. Really, is it not surprising how certain of our fellow-countrymen behave when they come abroad? Who would suppose, by his goings on, that he was a churchwarden at Peckham? No one, indeed, would assume that Jones in the atmosphere of London would take on so austere a job as the duties of a churchwarden. Here, in the atmosphere of Dieppe, on the French side of the Channel, he is the life and soul of a gay little band that haunts the Casino and turns night into day, besides betraying a most unholy delight in the society of female butterflies.

Unknown either to the correspondent or the editor of the *Sunday Chronicle*, there was a real Artemus Jones who was a barrister on the North Wales circuit, and a copy of the newspaper containing the article was handed to him whilst he was sitting in court at Chester Assizes. Although he was neither married nor was a churchwarden at Peckham, Artemus Jones was subsequently able to produce a number of witnesses from North Wales who knew him or knew of him and thought he was the person referred to. This was in the action for libel which he brought against E. Hulton & Co., the printers, proprietors and publishers of the *Sunday Chronicle*, and which was heard by Mr Justice Channell and a special jury at Manchester Assizes. In this instance, the judge directed the jury that the writer's actual intentions were irrelevant: the question was, would the ordinary reader think that the Peckham churchwarden was imaginary or was a real person called Artemus Jones? The jury had no doubts and returned a verdict for the plaintiff with £1,750 damages, the foreman adding that they were quite unanimous. Hulton's appealed and the Court of Appeal dismissed the appeal by two to one. Hulton's then went to the House of Lords, where four Law Lords were unanimous in rejecting the appeal, although they differed in their reasons, one view being that it was enough that the libel might be understood by ordinary readers to refer to Artemus Jones, and the other being that the newspaper had acted so recklessly in not bothering to find out whether such a person as Artemus Jones existed or not that their conduct should be regarded as a deliberate intention to libel him. It was therefore difficult to know exactly what the law on the subject of unintentional defamation was, where the newspaper could not be accused of acting with the same degree of negligence as the *Sunday Chronicle* was assumed to have done in the Artemus Jones case.

One result of the case was clear. In the words of Lord Chief Justice Goddard, it 'added a new terror to authorship'. Publishers became increasingly uneasy, and novelists were at pains to state at the beginning of their novels that all their characters were fictitious and that any resemblance to a living person was a pure coincidence, although this customary disclaimer did not really afford them any protection if sued for libel as the law then stood. Thus, until the change in the law took place by the Act of 1952, *Hulton* v. *Jones* remained the authority for the legal ruling that in an action for libel it is no defence to show that the defendant did not intend to defame the plaintiff, if reasonable people would think the language to be defamatory of him or her.[7]

The second case, which the Porter Committee had in mind, *Newstead* v. *London Express Newspaper Ltd*, arose out of a truthful statement made about an existing person with the same name. In 1939, the *Daily Express* ran a story about one Harold Newstead, a barman from Camberwell, who had been convicted of bigamy at the Old Bailey.

> Harold Newstead, 30-year-old Camberwell man, who was gaoled for nine months, liked having two wives at a time. Married legally for a second time in 1932 – his legal wife is pictured right, above – he unlawfully married 19-year-old Doris Skelly (left above). He said, 'I kept them both till the police interfered.'

This description was true as regards the Camberwell barman. But there was another Harold Newstead who was a hairdresser, assisting his father in business in Camberwell, and he sued the newspaper for libel alleging that the words were understood by a number of people to refer to him and to mean that he had committed bigamy, and that he had been punished for it, and that he was a person of no moral or social sense, 'unworthy of the confidence or trust of anyone, and especially of any woman, and that he was totally unfit to be a ladies' hairdresser.' The trial judge put three questions to the jury which they answered as follows:

> In omitting the occupation of the convicted man were the defendants (a) reckless, (b) negligent? – Negligent but not reckless.
>
> Damages, if any? – One farthing.
>
> Would reasonable persons understand the words complained of to refer to Harold Newstead the hairdresser?

The jury could not agree on the last question and were discharged. Who was entitled to judgment? The matter came before the Court of Appeal, and an order was made for a new trial on the ground that the plaintiff was entitled to have the third of the above questions answered by a jury, this in fact being the test laid down by the House of Lords in the Capital & Counties Bank case. History does not relate whether there was a new trial, but in making their order the appellate court held as a general principle that the fact that the words complained of were true of another person of the same name did not afford a good defence to an action for defamation.[8]

The third case cited by the Porter Committee related to a Press photograph of a man and a woman at a race meeting, the picture being accompanied by a caption which was on the face of it quite harmless but which by reason of facts unknown either to the photographer or the newspaper, which published the photograph, defamatory of the man's wife.[9] In 1928 a racehorse owner who went by the name of Corrigan, but whose real name was Cassidy, was photographed at his own request at Hurst Park races with a young woman who he told the photographer was his fiancée and who did not deny this. The *Daily Mirror* published the picture above the caption:

> Mr. M. Corrigan, the racehorse owner, and Miss X, whose engagement has been announced.

Michael Cassidy *alias* Corrigan was a colourful character, who had at one time been a general in the Mexican Army. He was also married but living apart from his wife, though he used to visit her from time to time in the suburb where she kept a shop. When her neighbours saw the picture they recognized Corrigan as the man who used to visit her as her husband and they jumped to the conclusion that Mrs Cassidy was not the respectable married woman she claimed to be but really had been living in open adultery with the man she claimed was her husband. Mrs Cassidy issued a writ for libel against the *Daily Mirror* on the ground that the publication in the newspaper meant that she was a dissolute and immoral woman who had imposed on her friends and acquaintances. The newspaper pleaded that in their natural and ordinary meaning the words of the caption were true, since Corrigan and the girl had proclaimed their engagement. The trial judge ruled that the words were capable of a defamatory meaning; the jury found that they were in fact defamatory of Mrs Cassidy and awarded her £500 damages. The Court of Appeal by two to one upheld both the trial judge's ruling and the jury's verdict, the jury having found that the words together with the photograph conveyed to reasonably minded people an aspersion on the plaintiff's moral character.

The implication of this case was well expressed by Lord Justice Greer in his dissenting judgment when he said:

> If the decision of my brethren in this case is right, it would be right to say that I could be successfully sued for damages for libel, if having been introduced to two apparently respectable people as persons engaged to be married, I repeated the statement in a letter to a friend, on the ground that my words meant that a lady unknown to me, who was in fact the wife of the man, was not his wife and was living in immoral intercourse with him . . .
>
> I am afraid that for the future people will have to walk with wary steps through life and hesitate a long time before they accept the assertion of anyone, whom they have known as a bachelor, that he is in truth a single man.

However, the law of unintentional defamation was clear enough. As the Victorian judge Lord Coleridge put it, 'it does not signify what the writer meant. The question is whether the alleged libel was so published by the defendant that the world would apply it to the plaintiff.'[10] It was later summarized by Lord Justice Scrutton, one of the majority judges in the Cassidy case, in the interesting action brought by a Russian princess against an American film company.[11]

> Though the person who writes and publishes the libel may not intend to libel a particular person and, indeed, has never heard of that particular person, the plaintiff, yet, if evidence is produced that reasonable people, knowing some of the circumstances, not necessarily all, would take the libel complained of to relate to the plaintiff, an action for libel will lie.

The limits of unintentional defamation were underlined in a recent case where the plaintiff pleaded that he had been libelled by innuendo, although the publication complained of did not refer to him either by name or description.[12]

In 1965 an ex-professional boxer and wrestler turned journalist named Johnny Morgan, in the course of collecting material on a dog doping gang story, took into his charge a kennel girl who told him and the police of the dog doping and her part in it. As she was to be a key witness in any prosecution of the gang, he put her into lodgings under surveillance while investigations proceeded. On 26 October she left the lodgings and spent the next six days at Morgan's flat. She was seen with him in public, and in particular on 28 October when six persons, who saw her in a state of distress, were introduced to her by Morgan and spoke to her. On 1 November Morgan took her into his charge until after the trial and conviction of some of the gang. On 7 November Morgan published his story in the *People*, a popular Sunday newspaper owned by Odham's. This contained an indistinct photograph of the kennel girl with her name underneath.

Next day, the *Sun*, a daily, also owned by Odham's, published a 'follow-up' article by a journalist named Peter Campling with the heading:

Dog doping girl goes into hiding.

The article stated among other things that she had been kidnapped in the previous week by members of the gang and kept in a house in Finchley. The article made no reference to the plaintiff either by name or description.

Morgan brought an action for libel against Odham's and Campling, claiming that he had been libelled by innuendo and called the six witnesses who had seen him with the girl. All the witnesses deposed that they thought the article referred to Morgan. In the result the jury found for the plaintiff and awarded him £4,750 damages. It was held on appeal that no one reading the article with care could reasonably think that the plaintiff Morgan was accused of being a kidnapper or involved in doping, that the witnesses had reached their conclusion not from the article but from their knowledge of the facts, and that the defendants therefore were entitled to succeed. In his judgment, Lord Denning, Master of the Rolls, said:

> To be capable of being understood to refer to a particular individual there had to be some key or pointer in the article itself indicating that it referred to him. Otherwise the limits of libel actions would be quite unreal.

During the forty years or so following the House of Lords decision in *Hulton* v. *Jones*, many cases of unintentional defamation were settled out of court by newspapers and publishers with apologies and money payments in order to avoid the risk of the additional expense of a trial. Some of them were undoubtedly of the 'gold-digging' variety. Fortunately, as a result of the 1952 Act, these are now a thing of the past. Under this Act anyone who 'innocently' publishes words defamatory of another person may escape liability for damages, but he must show that he 'exercised all reasonable care in relation to the publication', and also that he did not intend to defame the other person or that his words were not defamatory on the face of them, and that in either case he was ignorant of the circumstances by virtue of which they might be understood to refer to that other person. The Act further provides for the making of 'an offer of amends' in the shape of 'a suitable correction' and 'a sufficient apology'. Also, where the book or journal or other document has been distributed, reasonably practical steps must be taken to notify those who have received copies, e.g. retail booksellers or newsagents, that they contain allegedly defamatory matter. Where the offer is not accepted by the aggrieved party, this is a good defence provided the defendant can show that they were published 'innocently' and that the offer was made as soon as practicable after the complaint had been received and furthermore that the offer had not been withdrawn.

Thus the conditions which a defendant in a case of unintentional defamation has to satisfy in order to avoid having to pay damages are quite stringent. In the light of past experience it is as well that they should be.

III

The Porter Committee considered a number of other proposals, besides those relating to unintentional defamation. These were to the effect that the law should be extended to embrace defamation of the dead, invasions of privacy by the Press, and false statements vilifying groups or classes of persons distinguishable by race, colour, creed or vocation. 'In so far as abuses of these kinds call for remedy,' the Committee reported, 'we do not consider that any appropriate remedy falls within the general scope of the law of defamation.' However, they would appear to merit some brief notice here.

In the matter of race relations, Parliament has already stepped in to protect coloured members of the community from discrimination by the Race Relations Acts. On the other hand, the law governing the invasion of privacy, which constitutes in one sense an extension of the law of libel in many of the United States of America, finds little or no counterpart in Britain. The question has usually arisen where Press reporters have intruded upon those who have suffered some bereavement or have been connected with criminals or other notorious characters, and details of the private lives and affairs of such persons have been published by newspapers in sensational form with accompanying photographs. Normally it is not defamatory under English law to use a person's name without his authority or to publish his photograph or likeness without his consent, however much annoyance these acts may cause to his personal feelings. But the context or circumstances of such use or publication *may* cause it to convey a defamatory imputation.

The leading case on this aspect of the law is *Tolley* v. *Fry*, which arose from an advertisement published by the defendant company, which manufactured chocolate, in the form of a caricature of the amateur golf champion Cyril Tolley, who was shown with a packet of the defendants' chocolate protruding from his pocket as he played a stroke and listened to a caddie's doggerel verse in praise of Fry's product. As an amateur Mr

Tolley was not allowed to advertise, whether for payment or not, and he sued the chocolate manufacturers on the ground that their advertisement prostituted his reputation as an amateur golfer. At the trial the judge ruled that the advertisement was capable of a defamatory meaning, and the jury found that in fact it was a libel and awarded Tolley £1,000 damages. Fry's appealed on the ground that the trial judge's ruling was wrong and that the case should have been withdrawn from the jury, and furthermore that the damages were excessive. The Court of Appeal upheld the appeal.

> I have no hesitation in saying [remarked Lord Justice Greer] that in my judgment the defendants in publishing the advertisement in question, without first obtaining Mr. Tolley's consent, acted in a manner inconsistent with the decencies of life, and in doing so they were guilty of an act for which there ought to be a legal remedy. But unless a man's photograph, caricature or name be published in such a context that the publication can be said to be defamatory within the law of libel, it cannot be made the subject-matter of complaint by action at law.

Tolley in turn appealed to the House of Lords, which reversed the judgment of the Court of Appeal and restored the judge's ruling and the jury's verdict in the court of first instance, except that a new trial was ordered on the question of damages only. The advertisement was therefore finally held to be capable of conveying a defamatory imputation.[13] By way of contrast, in some jurisdictions in the United States the mere publication of a photograph of a person without his authority or consent for advertising purposes is an unlawful invasion of his right of privacy for which an action for damages or an injunction will lie without proof of special damage. Consequently some American commentators have considered that *Tolley* v. *Fry* involves a recognition of the right of privacy in England; but they ignore the vital fact that Tolley was an amateur golfer and the imputation was that he had been guilty of conduct unworthy of his amateur status in consenting to the publication of the advertisement.

Thus some infringements of individual privacy fall within the framework of defamation, provided they involve 'publication'. A comparatively recent case in point was *Fry* v. *Daily Sketch*, where the plaintiff who had been unhappily married received on settlement of libel proceedings substantial damages in respect of two articles about her marriage which gave the impression that she as 'so lacking in sensitivity, dignity and reserve' that she was prepared to authorize the publication of 'intimate, private and confidential information affecting her marriage and her family'.[14] In that case the plaintiff had also been subjected to persistent telephone calls and banging on her front door. The articles carried the heading

My Marriage
by Mrs. Jeremy Fry

and one of the articles was accompanied by a photograph with the caption:

Mrs. Fry is seen dancing with a friend at a recent ball.

It was stated in court that the publication of these articles had caused considerable distress and embarrassment to Mrs Fry and she was obliged to bring these proceedings to demonstrate that she was in no way the author of what had been published about her. Although the actual amount of the damages in settlement was not disclosed, it included the sum of £3,050 already paid into court by the defendants.

An action for defamation may also be an appropriate remedy where a person has suffered damage as the result of inaccurate statements about his credit-worthiness. The position is complicated by the role of mercantile agencies or trade protection societies which carry on the business of collecting information as to the credit and financial standing of other persons and selling it to traders and others who may or may not be members of the agency or society. Here the law has to steer a middle course between allowing third parties to help a tradesman to protect himself against dealing with insolvent persons and safeguarding commercial credit against unsubstantiated statements based on mere rumour.

If a person may legitimately inquire as to the character or credit of another – and there is no doubt that he is entitled to do so with regard to another person with whom he contemplates entering into trade relations – it follows that he is justified in making the inquiry through an agent confidentially employed for that purpose. In such a case the agent 'is under a legal duty to communicate the result of his inquiries to the person who has employed him to make them, and his duty is the basis of a distinct privilege arising out of the relationship of principal and agent'. Thus where a member of a trade protection association applied to the secretary for information as to the commercial credit of a trader with whom he proposed to deal, and the secretary having applied to X for the information and, having received a report, sent a report in substantially the same terms to the member, it was held that the secretary in making the inquiry and report was acting, not as the agent of the association, but as the confidential agent of the particular member, and that the 'publication' was therefore made on a privileged occasion. An action for defamation of character brought in these circumstances by the trader against the trade protection association therefore failed.[15]

The law on the matter is not settled. While it appears to allow the defence of privilege in the circumstances of such a case as that just cited, it does not allow this defence to credit agencies which are prepared to inquire about and sell their information to every kind of third party. The reason for this was well put by a great English lawyer, Lord Macnaghten, in a case decided in 1908, when he remarked that it was not in the interests of the community or the welfare of society that 'the protection which the law throws around communications made in legitimate self-defence or from a bona fide sense of duty should be extended to communications made from motives of self-interest by persons who trade for profit in the characters of other people.'[16]

The Porter Committee came to the conclusion that invasion of privacy was not a matter for which a suitable remedy could be found by an extension of the existing law of libel.

> The offence is primarily one against good taste, and if a legal remedy has to be created, it must, we think, lie in a sphere which is outside our terms of reference.

A legal remedy was indeed created in the form of the Press Council before which complaints of the invasion of privacy and other alleged unethical journalistic conduct are heard; but the utmost the Council can do is to administer a reprimand to the offending journal where no other wrong such as libel or trespass is involved. 'We ought to have in our law a right of action for infringement of privacy,' Lord Denning, the Master of the Rolls, has said recently. 'In the United States there has already been developed at common law a right of action for infringement of privacy.[17] We can only do it at the moment under cover of libel, as in Mr. Tolley's case.' The Lord Chancellor, Lord Gardiner, agreed; but, as he pertinently added, 'when one comes to sit down to try to compose it and put into words what exactly are the circumstances which constitute a breach of privacy, one realizes it is rather easier said than done.'[18]

Similarly with the defamation of the dead. The essence of civil proceedings for defamation is the damage caused to the reputation of the plaintiff, resulting in his being lowered in the estimation of his fellows. Any right to sue is regarded as a purely personal one and dies with him; it cannot be transferred to his estate or surviving relatives. Thus under English law, statements about the dead, however false and malicious they may be and however much distress they may cause to friends and relatives of the deceased, cannot form the subject of a civil action, nor of a criminal prosecution except to a very limited degree. (It is otherwise in Australia, if the words are likely to injure a relative's reputation or 'induce other persons to shun, or avoid, or ridicule, or despise him', and in Italy, where the conception of violation of family honour has been imported into the Italian Penal Code from Roman Law.) The question was considered by the Porter Committee, which was not disposed to recommend any change in the existing law. More recently it has come into public prominence through the publication of the German dramatist Rolf Hochhuth's play, *The Soldiers*, where the author charged Sir Winston Churchill when Prime Minister in the last war of allowing the death of the Polish General Sikorski in an aeroplane accident to be deliberately engineered. Churchill's family, though greatly pained by this baseless accusation, had no legal redress. It is conceivable that they might have publicly denounced the author as a liar and a coward in the hope of forcing him to take action against them for libelling him and the whole matter could have been aired in court, as was the case when the English Liberal leader Gladstone was accused of sexual immorality in a book by Captain Peter

Wright, and Gladstone's eldest son compelled the defamer to sue him in a remarkable trial in 1927. But, unlike Captain Wright, Hochhuth was not resident in England, and it is doubtful whether he would have responded in the manner desired.*

On the other hand, it can be – or at least it formerly could be – a crime to libel a dead person if it is done with the intention of injuring and bringing contempt on his family and so provoking them to a breach of the peace. In 1734 a man named Critchley was convicted of libelling Sir Charles Nicoll, K.B., who had been a member of Parliament, in an obituary notice stating that the dead man 'could not be called a friend of his country, for he changed his principles for a red ribbon and voted for that pernicious project the excise'. The innuendo was that Nicoll had obtained a knighthood 'by scandalous means, thereby reflecting on the Government which has the distribution of honours', and so Critchley was properly charged with defaming Nicoll and intending by his words 'to stir up the hatred and evil will of the subjects of the King against the family and posterity of the said Sir Charles.'

In 1789 the third Earl Cowper died in Florence, where he had spent most of his life collecting art treasures. He was known to be a man of homosexual habits. Writing about him in a newspaper shortly after his death, a journalist named Topham stated that his Lordship 'had led a wicked and profligate course

* Captain Edward Prchal, the Czech pilot who flew the plane which crashed, sued the licensees of the London theatre where the play ran for four months. 'As Sir Winston is dead, he cannot vindicate his reputation,' said the plaintiff's counsel in court. 'Mr. Prchal, however, can and does seek immediate redress by bringing the present proceedings.' These resulted in an agreed award of 'substantial damages' in an undisclosed amount and an unqualified apology. At the same time the defendants' counsel stated: 'The defendants welcome the opportunity of publicity acknowledging that they never believed there was any truth in, or foundation for, the suggestions made against either Mr. Prchal or Sir Winston and that their only desire was to preserve the freedom of the theatre whereby the public were afforded the opportunity of seeing plays however controversial they might be. In the circumstances, however, they regretted that their theatre should have been used for the publication of a serious and, in their view, wholly unfounded libel concerning Mr. Prchal, upon whose honour and reputation it was never the defendants' intention or desire to cast any reflection whatever.' *Prchal* v. *Albery and Others*, *The Times*, 1 August 1970.

of life, and had addicted himself to the practice and use of the most criminal and unmanly vices and debaucheries'. Topham was prosecuted at the suit of the Cowper family and convicted of publishing a criminal libel: but the verdict was set aside on the technical ground that there was no allegation in the indictment that the libel had been published 'with an intent to create any ill-blood or to throw any scandal on the family and posterity of Lord Cowper, or to induce them to break the peace vindicating the honour of the family.'

In the course of his judgment in the Topham case, Lord Chief Justice Kenyon had this to say:[19]

> To say, in general, that the conduct of a dead person can at no time be canvassed: to hold that, even after ages are passed, the conduct of bad men cannot be contrasted with good, would be to exclude the most useful part of history. And therefore it must be allowed that such publications may be made decently and honestly. But let this be done, whether soon or late after the death of the party, if it be done with a malevolent purpose, to vilify the memory of the deceased, and with a view to injure his posterity, as in *R.* v. *Critchley* . . . then it is done with a design to break the peace and then it becomes illegal.

Lord Kenyon's words were echoed by the Porter Committee a century and a half later when they recommended that it was not in the public interest that the law should be altered in this context.[20]

> Historians and biographers should be free to set out facts as they see them and to make their comment and criticism upon the events which they have chronicled. But to produce the strict proof of their statements contained in their writings, which the English law of evidence requires, becomes increasingly difficult with the lapse of time. If those engaged in writing history were compelled, for fear of proceedings for libel, to limit themselves to events of which they could provide proof acceptable to a Court of law, records of the past would, we think, be unduly and undesirably curtailed.

Thereafter prosecutions for libelling the dead eventually

became obsolete. The last reported case was tried at Cardiff Assizes in 1887 by the great criminal judge and historian of the English criminal law Sir James FitzJames Stephen. A popular local shipbuilder and merchant, one John Batchelor, who was the first chairman of the Cardiff School Board, died leaving considerable debts, and his friends proposed to erect a public statue in his memory. A solicitor of the town named Ensor wrote to the *Western Mail* suggesting that the following epitaph be inscribed on it:

> In honour of John Batchelor, a native of Newport, who in early life left his country for his country's good; who on his return devoted his life and energies to setting class against class, a traitor to the Crown, a reviler of the aristocracy, a hater of the clergy, a panderer to the multitude; who as first Chairman of the Cardiff School Board, squandered funds to which he did not contribute; who is sincerely mourned by unpaid creditors to the amount of £50,000; who at the close of a wasted and misspent life died a pauper, this monument, to the eternal disgrace of Cardiff, is erected by sympathetic Radicals.
>
> Owe no man anything.

It is difficult to conceive of a more flagrant example of a libel on a dead person calculated to cause 'a breach of the peace'. Indeed this one actually did so, since after its appearance in the local newspaper the late Mr Batchelor's outraged sons personally assaulted the author. They then proceeded to prosecute him for criminal libel. Nevertheless Mr Justice Stephen directed the jury to acquit Ensor on the ground that there was no evidence that the defendant intended to provoke or annoy the sons, and that 'a mere tendency to provoke or constructive intention inferred from the fact that the libel was calculated to hurt the feelings of any surviving relations was not enough.' This the jury did.

In the judge's view another of the essential conditions for founding a successful prosecution had not been established in this case.[21]

> There must be vilifying of the deceased with a view to injure his posterity [he declared]. The dead have no rights

> and can suffer no wrongs. The living alone can be the subject of legal protection, and the law of libel is intended to protect them not against every writing which gives them pain, but against writings holding them up individually to hatred, contempt or ridicule. . . . I am reluctant in the highest degree to extend the criminal law [of libel]. *To speak broadly, to libel the dead is not an offence known to our law.* If an extension of it is required it is for Parliament and not the judges to extend it.

And so the matter remains.

IV

Something further should be said on what may be conveniently described as group defamation – that is to say, 'false statements vilifying not identifiable individuals, but groups or classes of persons distinguishable by race, colour, creed or vocation.' Under the existing law, such statements cannot form the subject of civil proceedings for libel or slander. 'If a man wrote that all lawyers were thieves,' as a Victorian judge once put it, 'no particular lawyer could sue him unless there was something to point to the particular individual.'[22] Similarly, in the United States, where the Girl Scouts of America organisation recently filed a defamation suit claiming a million dollars (£416,000) against the Personality Poster Manufacturing Co. of New York in respect of a poster showing a girl scout in an advanced state of pregnancy and the scout motto 'Be Prepared', which it was alleged was 'intended to impute unchastity and moral turpitude to members', and to suggest that the scout motto encouraged the practice of contraception.[23] 'These strong allegations are bald allegations,' said New York District Court Judge Lasker in refusing to grant an injunction restraining the defendant company from continuing to display the poster, 'and the record is bare of any evidence that the plaintiff's reputation has been or is likely to be affected in any way by the wry, perhaps unmannerly behaviour of the defendant.' In view of this ruling, the Girl Scouts did not proceed with their case.

On the other hand, criminal proceedings will lie at common

law in England if the tendency of the words is 'to excite the angry passions' of the body or class libelled, or of the general public against the body or class, and so lead to a breach of the peace. Thus, as long ago as the reign of George II, where the defendant wrote and published of 'certain Jews lately arrived from Portugal and living near Broad Street' in the City of London that they had burnt a Jewish woman and her child because the father was a Christian, as a result of which Jews in the neighbourhood were 'attacked by the mob, barbarously treated and threatened with death in case they were found "abroad" any more', the court overruled the defendant's objection that no proceedings for criminal libel could lie 'because it did not appear who in particular the persons reflected on were.'[24] Similar proceedings were authorized early in the nineteenth century against the publishers of a newspaper for a libel reflecting upon the clergy of the Church of England, though no individual prosecutor was named.[25] The common law has now been statutorily reinforced by the Race Relations Acts of 1965 and 1968, which make it an offence to stir up racial hatred and to discriminate against 'any section of the public in Great Britain distinguished by colour, race, or ethnic or national origins', notably in the matter of housing employment and the provision to the public of goods, facilities and services. Unfortunately the Acts do not apply to Northern Ireland where religious discrimination against Roman Catholics in these respects is notorious.

Another matter which was considered by the Porter Committee and subsequently raised during the debates on the Defamation Bill in Parliament in 1952 was the proposal to get rid of the distinction between libel and slander by making all defamatory statements whether written or oral actionable *per se* in preference to continuing the requirement of having to prove special damage in most slander actions. It was argued (and indeed was accepted by a minority of the Committee) that no adequate reason existed for perpetuating a distinction which originated by an accident of English legal history, finds no place in Scots law, and has led to a confusing amount of case law over the years. The question had also been considered by the House of Lords Select Committee in 1843, which in addition to the Tory Lord Chancellor Lyndhurst and the former Whig

Lord Chancellor Brougham included Lords Abinger, Campbell, Cottenham and Langdale. As Lord Jowitt was to put it over a century later, 'anybody who knows the history of those times will think it absolutely amazing that Lyndhurst, Brougham, Campbell and Cottenham can have agreed on any single proposition. But they did.' In fact, they agreed that the distinction between libel and slander should be abolished and they carried the rest of the Committee with them, pointing out among other anomalies that 'falsely and maliciously to impute in the coarsest terms and on the most public occasions . . . want of veracity or courage to a gentleman of undoubted honesty and honour cannot be the foundation of any proceeding civil or criminal; whereas an action may be maintained for saying that a cobbler is not skilful in mending shoes.' Thus they reported that the distinction between libel and slander did not rest on any solid foundation and recommended that 'whenever an injury is done to character by defamation there ought to be redress by action.'[26] However, the proposal was not acceptable to Parliament and consequently found no place in the Libel Act passed in the same year. Nor was it acceptable either to the majority of the Porter Committee or to that in Parliament in 1952, apparently for the same reason in each instance, namely the fear of a multiplicity of slander actions resulting from such a change in the law. The Porter Committee reported:[27]

> Slander is often trivial, not infrequently good-tempered and harmless, and in that form commonly enough a topic of conversation. If all slander were actionable *per se*, the scope for trivial but costly litigation might be enormously increased. So far as slander in ordinary conversation is concerned, it is not normally taken seriously by speaker or listener, and, in the great majority of cases, does little or no harm.

Academic legal opinion has long been in favour of assimilating the two branches of the law in England, and in his speech on the Second Reading of the Defamation Bill in 1952 Jowitt cited in particular the views of Professors Holdsworth, Winfield and Goodhart in support of the change.[28] Jowitt also mentioned a personal experience.

> I remember the case of the headmaster of a famous public school who had retired from the school owing to illness. He came back after about a year, and found that there was a rumour going about that he had misconducted himself with some woman of the town, and all sorts of details were given. It was wholly untrue. It was most damaging to this man.
>
> He came to me and asked my advice about bringing an action. I told him: 'You can do absolutely nothing. If you retired and these people said that the real reason for your retirement was that you were "kicked out" by the council for your bad behaviour, you could do nothing.'

'Is that right or is that just?' asked Jowitt. 'I submit that the time has come when this thing ought to be altered.'

But the majority of his fellow peers did not agree, nor did the Commons, where the measure originated as a Private Members' Bill, and Jowitt was unable to obtain any effective support there for his view, not even from Sir Hartley Shawcross and Sir Frank Soskice (as they then were) who had been the Law Officers in the first post-war Labour Government when Jowitt was Lord Chancellor. The conventional view, which Parliament adopted, was expressed by Lord Porter himself, not only in the report which is usually known by his name but also in the speech he made in the debate immediately following Jowitt, that 'there might arise a large number of unnecessary claims, even slight questions of quarrels between neighbours over the fence, which I have known to happen.' He recalled a case which he had tried in which he would have awarded something between one farthing and £5, 'the man having some right'. But there was a very sympathetic jury, and 'with all my endeavours' Porter could not prevent the jury from giving him £100.

> It is that class of case which one is anxious should not occur in this country. It is all very well to say that Scotland does not do it. Scottish juries do not give large sums. Someone once said that the Scots are a cautious nation – cautious in what they say and in what they do. I do not think it is fair to say that because one system acts with one nation it will act with another. After all, we have

for many years put up with the distinction, and it has not worked badly.

The same kind of argument was used in the House of Lords in the previous century when it was proposed to abolish hanging for sheep-stealing and other petty thefts. It is extremely doubtful today whether the change really would produce a flood of trivial slander actions. The costs alone of bringing an action should be sufficient to deter the frivolous litigant, and it should be borne in mind that the parties in defamation actions do not qualify for state 'legal aid', such proceedings being expressly exempted by the statute. On the other hand, there are advocates of the extension of legal aid to defamation cases, particularly where there are 'reasonable grounds' for taking proceedings, but it may well be that the judicial discretion exercised in deciding whether or not to grant a certificate of legal aid should be sufficient to meet all objections both to the proposal to assimilate the law of libel and slander and to the proposal to include defamation actions within the field of legal aid.

Today the gravest criticisms of the English law of defamation are on the ground of increasing procedural technicality and expense. A recent action, colloquially known as 'The Case of the Three Little Pigs' and described by Lord Justice Diplock as 'an ordinary simple case of libel', took fifteen days to try, the summing up lasted for a whole day and the jury returned thirteen special verdicts. The notice of appeal set out seven separate grounds why the appeal should be allowed and ten more why a new trial should be granted, the latter being split up into forty separate sub-grounds. The respondent's notice contained fifteen separate grounds why the appeal should not be allowed. 'The costs must be enormous,' commented the judge. 'Lawyers should be ashamed that they have allowed the law of defamation to have become bogged down in such a mass of technicalities that this should be possible.'[29] As the learned editors of the latest edition of *Gatley on Libel and Slander* have pointed out, such result may deter a worthy plaintiff from bringing an action even when he has a good case, or, equally, encourage an unscrupulous plaintiff to do so even when he has not. 'Either innocent men lose their reputations or proper comment is stifled. Neither outcome is to the public good.'[30]

One highly technical aspect of the law of defamation is afforded by the question of malice when pleaded in the ordinarily understood sense of the term as meaning ill-will. Malice can be, and often is, alleged by the plaintiff to rebut the defence of fair comment or privileged communication, but as the law stands at present the plaintiff need not give particulars in the pleadings (which are exchanged by the parties before the case comes into court) of the facts, other than the terms of the alleged defamatory words or matter themselves, upon which he will rely as giving rise to the inference that the defendant was actuated by express malice. That a plaintiff in such a case should furnish these particulars was one of the recommendations of the Porter Committee which has not yet been implemented.[31] The defendants' leading counsel in the Liberace case, now Lord Gardiner, protested about it in his closing speech to the jury.[32] There is also the case of a publisher of a journal being unaware of malice on the part of a contributor of an article, which the publisher accepted in good faith for publication, and in the same context of the maligned person being ignorant of the contributor's identity where the article was unsigned. This question arose in the action brought by Mr Eugene Gros and Scientific Consultants Ltd against the editor and publisher of *The Times Literary Supplement* in respect of the review of a bibliography of Russian books on automation and computers compiled and published by the plaintiffs. The reviewer was not a party to the action, probably because it was not until a few days before the hearing began that his identity became known to the plaintiffs, for whom he had previously worked as a translator for some years. Nor was the editor aware of this connection until shortly before the case came into court. In the event the plantiffs won the action, the trial judge finding the reviewer guilty of malice and assessing the damages in all at £7,000 with costs.

In giving judgment in this case Mr Justice Blain added:[33]

> Time after time in actions for libel the hearings are so prolonged that the costs are inevitably out of all proportion to the damages, even substantial damages, that are or might be awarded. This must be a serious burden to the press and to other publishers, and for that matter to Plaintiffs waiting a year or so to have their reputations

vindicated in those cases where they succeed.

Much of this time and expense is due to the lack of clarity about a number of aspects of the law of defamation and lack of definite definition of principles which could be clearly defined. For one example I would think that publishers would welcome some statutory limitation, or at least clarification, of their liability for the malice of authors and contributors who alone can know how far their malicious statements are justifiable . . .

Likewise in cases where a defence is pleaded which can only be negatived by proof of malice, it might be considered that in this day and age, when we are more jealous to protect the innocent-minded publishers, a maligned person should be entitled to know the identity of one who may be a highly malicious and self-interested writer . . .

But I have no doubt that if Mr Gros had been informed of the author's identity as soon as he complained, his reputation would quickly have been cleared and the defendants would have been spared the main consequences of long, expensive, and unsuccessful litigation.

The Gros case affords a good example of the allegation of malice by a plaintiff, or rather a plaintiff's lawyers, being used successfully to rebut the defence of privilege by a newspaper when the fact of malice is unknown to the editor at the time. Conversely in the case of the 'Three Little Pigs' where it appeared that the jury intended to find malice but being somewhat confused found as a fact that the defendant had acted without malice, the judge held that the communication was privileged and the plaintiff consequently lost the action. The facts were as follows. A firm of auctioneers, W. S. Bagshaw & Sons, held a sale of livestock at Tutbury in Staffordshire. Three pigs were knocked down to a man wearing a brown smock, who gave his name as 'Boston of Rugeley', for £103 19s. He ought to have paid for the pigs before he took them away. But somehow he managed to get hold of them without paying for them and went off with them in a trailer. He was never seen again. He had stolen the pigs under a false name. The auctioneers informed the police and on the next day sent a circular letter to a number of other auctioneers in the area telling them of the circumstances of the theft. They also told the Chief Constable for the county, offering a reward of £25 for the recovery of the pigs, and asked if it would be possible to arrange for the matter to be put out on television. The Chief Constable accordingly arranged for a script about the missing pigs and the reward to appear on the local Associated Television programme. ('Three little piggies left the market on a trailer . . . in the care of a gentleman who said his name was Boston and he came from Rugeley . . . so if you know of anyone of that description who has just acquired three pedigree Wessex Saddleback Gilts, the £25 reward could be yours, or at least bacon for breakfast.') Now there was a farmer in Rugeley named Alfred Boston, quite unconnected with the thief. He sued the auctioneers and A.T.V. for libel claiming that the circular letter and the telecast, which went on for two days, were libels on him, as people had understood them to refer to him. The claim against A.T.V. was settled and at the trial judgment was given for the auctioneers as already stated.

On appeal it was held that both the letter and the telecast material were protected by privilege, and so far as the police were concerned, an innocent person affected by a police notice must endure the misfortune for the sake of the public good; also that, as the jury had found that the auctioneers were not actuated by malice and as the summing up by the trial judge was not unbalanced or unfair, the appeal must be dismissed. The appellate court likewise refused a motion for a new trial, although all twelve jurors had made affidavits indicating that they gave their answers to the trial judge under a misapprehension and that they would, if they could, change their answers so as to say that the auctioneers were actuated by malice. 'To my mind it is settled as well as anything can be that it is not open to the court to receive any such evidence as this,' said Lord Denning. 'Once a jury has given their verdict and it has been accepted by the judge and they have been discharged they are not at liberty to say they meant something different.'[34]

It was hardly surprising that the jury, who had been required by the trial judge to answer thirteen questions which he put to them and which resulted in thirteen 'special verdicts', should have been confused. 'I did not know whether I was on my head or my heels,' one juror was reported as having said afterwards. Another put it thus: 'I think the legal mumbo-jumbo beat us.' And so in a sense it had.

The jurors' comments on this case were quoted by the newspaper proprietor Lord Thomson of Fleet in a debate in the House of Lords in 1966 on the Press and the Law. The debate was initiated by Lord Tangley, a well-known solicitor, formerly Sir Edwin Herbert, and member of the inter-Party organization Justice, which had been considering the subject in detail, and had invited proposals for the reform of the law in this context. Lord Thomson, who owns *The Times*, the *Sunday Times* and hundreds of other journals, came forward with what he called 'two small reforms which could help'. One of these – that the Press should be given clear protection for fair and accurate reports of all foreign parliamentary and judicial proceedings – commanded general support. But the other – that juries should be abolished in libel actions – ran into considerable opposition with the lawyers in the Upper House.

> Libel actions should be tried by judges alone [said Lord Thomson]. Jurors may be excellent for criminal trials where they have to give simply 'guilty' and 'not guilty' verdicts. The law of libel is, however, different. It has become so technical that it is asking too much of juries to cope with its complexities . . . The result is that libel actions are a lottery and are apt to be decided other than on their true merits. A judge is much better qualified to deal with the technicalities, and a judge, I submit, is in a much better position to fix a proper figure for damages.

Lord Thomson did not say exactly why he thought a judge better in this respect, apart from objecting to the practice told him by one jury foreman of asking each member to write down the amount he or she would give on a piece of paper, adding them up and dividing the result by twelve. 'This is not a very scientific way of meting out justice,' commented Lord Thomson. However, he might have added that it is a peculiarly English way of doing so, and although it may have resulted in some uncomfortably large sums awarded against newspapers in the opinion of Press Lords, it is always open to the Court of Appeal to order a new trial on the ground that the damages are excessive.

A typical lawyer's reaction to the Thomson proposal came from Lord Conesford, a Tory Queen's Counsel, who thought it 'rather interesting that somebody with knowledge, at any rate of the Press, should be quite so ignorant of the history of this country and the importance of trial by jury' as to propose 'to cast aside something so embedded in our law since Fox's Libel Act of the 18th century as though it were a matter of trivial importance.' The point was rubbed in by the Master of the Rolls, Lord Denning, who reminded Lord Thomson that it was a jury in Fox's time, when directed by the Lord Chief Justice Lord Mansfield to find the printers and publishers of a certain newspaper guilty in a trial for criminal libel, who insisted on returning a verdict of not guilty. 'And if I may say so to the members of the Press,' added Lord Denning, 'the freedom of the Press in England was established by the jury.' Later in the debate the Lord Chancellor, Lord Gardiner, looking back on an outstandingly successful career as a barrister, particularly in libel and slander cases, recalled that he could hardly remember a single civil case in which he thought the jury were wrong. 'In criminal cases juries do acquit large numbers of guilty people,' he said, 'but in civil cases they get a sort of wisdom which is greater collectively than the wisdom of any one of them.' And, as Lord Tangley put it in winding up the debate, 'the traditional view of the Englishman is that when life or reputation is at stake, he would prefer to have it judged by twelve ordinary people rather than one man, however impartial or learned he may be. I think that that is the attitude which both the Press and the law must respect. I certainly do.' It is difficult to see Parliament abolishing juries in defamation cases in the present climate of opinion.

V

It remains to notice briefly the questions of damages and contempt of court in the context of defamation proceedings. In all actions for libel and in certain actions for slander, i.e. where proof of 'special damage' is unnecessary, as for instance are unjustified allegations of adultery or unchastity against a woman or girl, the plaintiff does not have to allege that actual damage has resulted from the words complained of. As one

Victorian judge put it, 'the law presumes that *some* damage will flow in the ordinary course of things from the mere invasion of his absolute right to reputation' and he is entitled to such general damages as the jury or the judge may properly find, although he proves no actual damage.[35] But where the words are actionable only on proof of special damage, as in the majority of slander cases, the plaintiff must expressly allege such damage, giving full particulars, otherwise his action will automatically fail. And, of course, in libel actions where the plaintiff adds a claim in respect of special damage to the primary claim for general damage, e.g. a general falling off of business, he must allege such damage with 'reasonable particularity'.

Damages in defamation cases have varied from 'the smallest coin of the realm', formerly a farthing, as when the art critic Ruskin described the artist Whistler as 'a coxcomb' who had the impudence to ask two hundred guineas 'for flinging a pot of paint in the public's face', to £50,000, the agreed damages awarded by the jury to Mr William Lever, M.P., later the first Viscount Leverhulme, against the *Daily Mail* and other newspapers controlled by Lord Northcliffe, for having persistently stated that Mr Lever had formed a soap trust to exploit the consumer by cornering the raw materials market and raising the price of his soap. 'There is no answer to this action for libel, and the damages must be enormous,' wrote F. E. Smith, later Lord Birkenhead, in a terse opinion he gave the plaintiff. This was in 1908. Although larger sums have been awarded, they have subsequently been reduced on appeal, and the award in the soap trust case is believed to constitute a record, particularly when it is borne in mind that the damages in respect of similar libels printed in other Northcliffe papers amounted in all to nearly £220,000. Other large sums given by juries to successful plaintiffs were £40,000 in the recent PQ 17 case, and £25,000 awarded to the late Princess Irene Youssoupoff against Metro-Goldwyn-Mayer Pictures in 1934 arising out of the film *Rasputin the Mad Monk*, in which the Princess was grossly misrepresented as Rasputin's mistress during the final period of the Tsarist monarchy in Russia.

The defendant company in the Youssoupoff case appealed on the ground that the damages were excessive, but the appeal failed and the court refused to order a new trial. In his judgment in the Court of Appeal Lord Justice Greer said:

> No doubt the damages are very large for a lady who lives in Paris, and who has not lost, so far as we know, a single friend, and who has not been able to show that her reputation has in any way suffered from the publication of this unfortunate picture play; but, of course, one must leave out of account a great many other things. One of them is that it is very difficult to value the reputation of any human being. It is very difficult to put a money figure upon the mental pain and suffering that is necessarily undergone by a good and delicate woman who has been foully libelled in the presence of large numbers of people.

In practice a new trial is seldom granted on the ground that the damages awarded are either too great or too small. One reason for this is that the Court of Appeal has not the advantage of seeing the witnesses and so being able to draw conclusions as to the quantum of damages from the evidence they give. On the other hand, the scope of punitive or exemplary damages has recently been limited by the House of Lords in the case of *Rookes* v. *Barnard* to actions where the defendant has expressly sought to profit financially by blackening the plaintiff's character.[36] Apart from the PQ 17 case (see Appendix II, pp. 176–9) no newspaper or publisher has been held to have done this. At present the Court of Appeal has power to vary damages awarded by a judge sitting without a jury, but in the case of a jury trial the appellate court can only order a new trial if it disagrees with the damages, but cannot either increase or decrease the amount awarded by the jury.

In recommendations made by the joint working party of Justice and the British Committee of the International Press Institute in their report *The Law and the Press*, published in 1965, it was proposed that the power of the Court of Appeal to vary the amount of damages should be extended to cases heard by juries. Other recommendations included a proposal to amend the Defamation Act of 1952 in the sense that, if the truth of every allegation of fact is not proved by the defendant in defamation proceedings, the defence shall not fail if the words not proved to be true do not materially affect the plaintiff's reputation taking the publication as a whole. It was also proposed that the question of whether it is contempt of court to publish a further libel after a writ has been issued or to comment on a libellous publication which has appeared elsewhere should be clarified in any future legislation.

The question of contempt was discussed in a recent case in which the judge ruled that the publication of a book about scientology, written by a Church of England rector, could prejudice the fair trial of forthcoming libel and slander actions involving the Church of Scientology of California and therefore amounted to a contempt.[37] The passage complained of in the book referred to an article in the *Sunday Times* alleging that the founder of the scientology movement, Mr L. Ron Hubbard, had once been involved in black magic. An action against the newspaper had been settled six months before the book was published, but the author stated, as he believed, that the dispute was still to be decided. The scientologists had asked the judge to commit the rector to prison for contempt and to penalize the publishers. However, during the hearing it was stated that the rector had not been served with notice of the proceedings and that the move to commit him would not be pressed. The judge declined to make any penalty order against the publishers, presumably because they had withdrawn the book from circulation pending the outcome of the hearing.

In spite of the increasing complications and expense in bringing a defamation action, certainly the law ought not to regard lightly injuries to a man's or a woman's character. It is for this reason that there seems no satisfactory basis in principle for excepting defamation cases from the benefits of the legal aid scheme. The invocation of the law and its remedies are movingly expressed by Shakespeare in Cassio's cry to Iago in *Othello*: 'I have lost my reputation! I have lost the immortal part of myself, and what remains is bestial!' The English law of defamation provides remedies which may or may not always be adequate, but which are full of complications and subtleties as this book reveals.

References

1 Baron Parke in *Carmiter* v. *Coupland* (1840) 6 M. and W., at p. 108.
2 *Johnson* v. *Browning* (1705). 6 Modern Reports, 217.
3 For details, see present writer's *The Trials of Oscar Wilde* (1948, 1962).
4 *Kerr* v. *Kennedy* [1942] 1 K.B. 109. The plaintiff was awarded £300 damages and costs.
5 Lord Penzance in *Capital & Counties Bank* v. *Henty* (1882) 7 Appeal Cases, at p. 762.
6 *Capital & Counties Bank* v. *Henty* (1882) 7 Appeal Cases, 741.
7 *Hulton* v. *Jones* [1910] A.C. 20.
8 [1940] 1 K.B. 377; 56 T.L.R. 130.
9 *Cassidy* v. *Daily Mirror Newspapers Ltd* [1929] 2 K.B. 331.
10 *Gibson* v. *Evans* (1889) 23 Q.B.D. 384.
11 *Youssoupoff* v. *Metro-Goldwyn-Mayer Pictures Ltd* (1934) 50 T.L.R. at p. 583.
12 *Morgan* v. *Odham's Press Ltd* [1970] 1 W.L.R. 820 C.A.
13 *Tolley* v. *Fry* [1930] 1 K.B. 467; [1931] A.C. 333.
14 *The Times* 29 June 1966.
15 *London Association for Protection of Trade* v. *Greenlands* [1913] 3 K.B. 507; [1916] 2 A.C. 15.
16 *Macintosh* v. *Dun* [1908] A.C. at p. 400.
17 For an excellent account of this branch of United States law, see Morris L. Ernst and Alan U. Schwartz, *Privacy: The Right to be Let Alone*, New York and London, 1962.
18 *House of Lords Debates*, vol. 274, cols. 1429–30, 1944 (25 May 1966). The Law Commission in its fourth annual report to the Lord Chancellor (December 1969) pointed out that the recent differences between the Press Council and the *News of the World* about the publication of the memoirs of Miss Christine Keeler, whose association with Mr John Profumo led to the latter's resignation as War Minister in 1963, had focused attention on the urgent need for an early examination of the law relating to privacy. Such an examination has recently been undertaken by Justice, the British Section of the International Commission of Jurists, in its Report *Privacy and the Law*, published in 1970.
19 *R.* v. *Topham* (1791) 4 Term Reports (Durnford and East) 126 at pp. 129–30.
20 Report, para. 29.
21 *R.* v. *Ensor* (1887) 3 T.L.R. 366. Author's italics.
22 Mr Justice Willes in *Eastwood* v. *Hilmes* (1858) 1 F. and F. at p. 349.
23 *Daily Telegraph*, 6 August 1969.
24 *R.* v. *Osborne* (1732) 2 Swanst. 503 n.
25 *R.* v. *Williams* (1822) 1 Dow and Ry, 197.
26 Cited by Lord Jowitt in debate on Defamation Bill; *House of Lords Debates*, vol. 177, cols. 1103–4 (15 July 1952).

27 Report, para. 38.
28 'If the rules applicable to libel were applied to all kinds of defamation, and the fact that the defamation was oral was only allowed to weigh in considering the measure of damages, no serious complaint could be made against our modern law'; W. S. Holdsworth, *A History of English Law*, VIII, 378.
29 *Boston* v. *Bagshaw* [1966] 1 W.L.R. 1126.
30 1967 edition, at p. viii.
31 Report, paras. 167–9.
32 In 1959 the American entertainer Liberace sued the *Daily Mirror* and its columnist William Connor ('Cassandra') for having described him as 'the summit of sex' and, among other epithets, as 'scent-impregnated' and 'fruit-flavoured', thereby suggesting that he was a homosexual. The jury awarded him £8,000 damages, having found the article complained of was neither true in fact nor fair comment.
33 *The Times*, 19 April 1969.
34 *Boston* v. *Bagshaw* [1966] 1 W.L.R. 1136.
35 Lord Justice Bowen in *Ratcliffe* v. *Evans* [1892] 2 Q.B. at p. 528.
36 [1964] A.C. 1129.
37 *The Times*, 31 July 1970. This case shows how the issue of a writ for libel can in effect constitute a form of literary censorship because of the risk of contempt proceedings.

Two

Freer Speech – and Privacy

Louis Blom-Cooper, Q.C.

Nothing short of the abolition of the civil right of action for libel will redress the balance between the public need for the greatest amount of discussion on matters of public interest and the protection of individual privacy. To complete the redressing process, a revival of the power to prosecute for criminal libel; a more effective Press Council; and a new right of action for invasion of privacy will be necessary. Such bald, not to say bold, proposals call for sustained argumentation. It is the purpose of this essay to justify so radical and novel a reform of the law.

Every libel is both a crime and a civil wrong. Indeed most crimes are civil wrongs; the exceptions are those statutory offences for which Parliament does not prescribe a civil remedy and the civil courts do not supply any cause of action. But, whereas unlawful behaviour attracts more frequently the criminal process, it is the reverse in the case of libel. Today a defamation statement evokes in the general public no sense of criminal responsibility but only the opportunity for the defamed to exact monetary compensation in the civil courts.

The prime reason for this almost exclusive preference for the civil process is that a criminal prosecution brings little personal satisfaction and no financial reward to the victim, whereas the civil action holds out the prospect of money being extracted from those who usually are of sufficiently substantial means to make them worthwhile pursuing through the courts. Defamatory statements have been the subject of criminal prosecutions only where the words uttered are so scurrilous or aggravated, either in their intrinsic gravity or in their public nature, that a civil remedy fails to afford the victim and the public any adequate means of stifling the repetition of the defamatory statements and of preventing public disorder. Clearly, a prosecution is not to be employed to curb or cure a mere verbal squabble between two individuals, however acrimonious and vindictive. But is it right that society should lend its aid, by providing a remedy in the civil courts, to provide the defamed with a right to monetary compensation out of the defamer's pocket?

Many a victim of the wounding word has uttered with Iago:

Good name in man and woman, dear my lord,
Is the immediate jewel of their souls;
Who steals my purse steals trash; 'tis something, nothing;
'Twas mine, 'tis his, and has been slave to thousands;
But he that filches from me my good name
Robs me of that which not enriches him,
And makes me poor indeed. (*Othello*, Act III, sc. 3)

But how many plaintiffs have protested from the witness box that they bring their actions for libel solely to vindicate their reputations and yet in the same breath eagerly enough accept the jury's award of damages? Has any plaintiff ever asked a jury simply to record a verdict in his favour but not to award him any damages? True, there have been frequent instances of plaintiffs announcing (and no doubt fulfilling their declared pronouncements) that damages will be paid to a charity. But few plaintiffs desire only to clear their good names and not at the same time at least to seek to punish their defamers by mulcting them in damages. Even those who are content to vindicate their reputations have the pleasure of receiving a grovelling apology read in open court, together with an order for costs usually on an indemnity basis.

Forgetting for the moment the hurt pride and reputation of the defamed, one might reasonably ask the question: if the opportunity for vindication of the defamed's reputation is all that the law is required to supply, is there not a case for abolishing the right to damages, or at least for substituting a less formalized, ritualistic and more effective method for achieving just that? One might ask an even more pertinent question: is the law of civil libel a real attempt to effect social control, or is it simply a relic of a legal system that functioned solely in property terms in seeking to provide compensation out of the wrongdoer's pocket for the victim's loss in reputation and social esteem?

It is common nowadays for both social scientists and lawyers to ask themselves whether or not a particular legal remedy achieves a desirable social objective. There is a growing body of opinion that deprecates the continuance of fault liability in personal injury cases: the reform proposed stems from the logical view that it is necessary that society should adequately reimburse the physical casualties of a highly organized industrial society for any actual loss suffered as a result of hospitalization or other incapacitating factor – but not out of the pocket of the person causing the injury, whether by fault or blamelessly.

The same approach is relevant here. Do we, by the agency of the civil law of libel, seek to prevent the purveyors of the written word from besmirching people's characters, or do we simply recognize that individuals are entitled to exact a monetary price from those who indulge their appetite for defamation? I want to suggest very strongly that the law of civil libel is largely unconcerned with the wider issue of social control and primarily, if not exclusively, focuses its attention on rewarding the defamed. I want to go further and argue that not only is this a one-dimensional (and hence lop-sided) view of the purpose of law, but that in its wake the law of libel operates in a manner that is positively inimical to the public weal.

That the law is interested in punishing the defamer is evidenced by the recent case of *Broome* v. *Cassell & Co. Ltd and Irving*, the PQ 17 case.[1] Ordinarily, the law seeks to deter potential defamers only by exacting compensatory damages. The fact is that the law countenances punitive or exemplary damages, over and above compensatory damages. Yet the punitiveness expressed by the law, and the penalty exacted, simply go to swell the defamed's pocket. Why? If money for libel is compensation, then the victim would receive what is deemed to be recompense, so far as a damaged reputation can ever be measured in money terms. There is no logic in giving the victim an extra dollop simply because his defamer is recalcitrant or strikes a poor figure in the jury's eyes. If the law desires to inflict a punitive sanction, over and above the amount to be paid as compensation, there is no morality in punitiveness benefiting the victim's bank account. I suspect that exemplary damages are an afterthought by the law which dislikes the more deliberate and outrageous defamations, and can hit out at the defamer only by delving more deeply into his pocket to the benefit of the only available beneficiary, the plantiff in the libel action. Perhaps the prime benefit from the PQ 17 case will be an awareness by the legal profession of the social inconsistencies of the present law of libel.

There are two other aspects of the present law of libel which agitate my mind. The first is the knowledge that many aspiring plaintiffs threaten libel proceedings like a timid swimmer uses his toe at the water's edge. They are testing the temperature, to see whether some tax-free bonus cannot be extracted from the publishers of a libel without having to run the gauntlet of the legal process. If someone could research the files of the members of the Newspaper Publishers' Association, there would, I suspect, be revealed some information about the extent (even enormity) of the gold-digging efforts of supposedly outraged potential plaintiffs. This kind of extraction of money, paid sensibly enough to buy off troublesome law suits, is nothing more than blackmail. And the law is the instrument whereby the blackmail is perpetrated. The law should not allow itself to be lent for so socially undesirable a practice.

The second aspect which induces an anti-social practice is the use to which the writ for libel is put by those who desire to fob off those investigating the writ-issuer's nefarious goings-on. It is a well known device of those who sail close to the wind (if not actually being caught up in some nasty squalls) that as soon as there is a breath of suspicion that their activities are to be revealed in a newspaper they issue a writ. Not only does this have the effect of threatening the newspaper with an action for libel, with all its attendant problems, but it also effectively stifles, for the protracted period while the legal process wends its weary way through the preparations for trial, all further communication of information relative to the defamatory matter. The *sub judice* rule is bandied about so as to provide extended cover to many a fraudsman. Here again the law's device for protecting its processes untainted by public comment is diverted to a wholly improper purpose. And if, strictly speaking, the *sub judice* rule cannot have such an all-embracing effect, there are few newspaper editors who are brave enough to spar with the judiciary.

A third disadvantage is the complementary power which a defamed plaintiff has of obtaining an interlocutory injunction against the publisher who threatens to continue spreading the particular gospel. It was once said by that great libel expert, Mr Justice Slade, that it was impossible for a plaintiff to obtain from the courts an injunction pending the trial of an action, because to grant it before the action is tried would be to prejudice the issue in favour of the plaintiff to the extent of abridging the defendant's right of free speech. That simplistic view, echoing the clarion words of the First Amendment to the United States Constitution, has everything to commend it.[2] But it does not represent the current law: interlocutory injunctions in libel actions can be, and are granted in suitable cases where repetition of the defamatory matter (which on the face of it discloses a fairly clear and serious libel) is threatened. I wonder what would happen if a candidate at a parliamentary election issued a writ for libel against his opponent and then sought an interlocutory injunction. Could he thus restrict his rival's campaigning? Fortunately, parliamentary candidates have the great good sense not to issue writs during an election: there are occasional exceptions. But would a court grant an interlocutory injunction in such circumstances? If so it would be a terrifying instrument for stifling political free speech.

There has in recent years been a movement to effect a change in the law of libel so as to free the Press from fear of proceedings in certain circumstances. The main proposal has been to confer a new form of qualified privilege where the newspaper can establish that all reasonable steps have been taken to ascertain the truth of what has been published. The proponents of this new defence recognize that the public is unwilling to concede to the Press any special legal protections, even if it were persuaded that some benefit would accrue to the public by the removal of the present inhibitions on the dissemination of news. Whatever the benefits, a protection of qualified privilege would, so the opponents' argument runs, make editors careless (or rather, carefree) of the protection from libels on innocent individuals. There is undoubtedly here a conflict of interest, between the duty of the Press to report matters of public interest and, on the other hand, the need to protect the individual beyond even the point of monetary compensation.

But Press demands for fewer legal inhibitions on its activities, on the one hand, and the protection of the individual, on the other hand, are neither antithetic nor irresoluble in terms of legal rules. The clue to the resolution of these apparently conflicting aims lies in the legitimate areas of activity. If the injuries inflicted on individuals by wounding statements in the Press can be divided into those where public interest properly belongs, and those restricted to matters of personal conduct devoid of anything but prurient curiosity, a line of resolution begins to open up. The formula is: leave the Press and other media of communication free to publish matters of public interest, unencumbered by any threats of libel damages (the criminal law would be the sole threat) and place a much tighter control (by way of a damper) on the publication of matters not within the public domain.

The critics of any proposal to abolish the civil law of libel would imediately retort that the withdrawal of any legal remedy in the civil courts to the defamed would be tantamount to a licence to tell lies. This, I fancy, is the crux of the argument in favour of the present law.

The removal of the sanction of the threat of libel damages would not, in my view, represent an invitation to editors and publishers to indulge themselves in grossly irresponsible publications. Indeed it would be a plea to them to use their new-found freedom in a more responsible way than has been sometimes the case in the past, and to restrict their unshackled freedom only in the public interest. To add to this, there is a strong suspicion that editors and publishers, with rather longer purses than some of their confrères in the publishing world, take calculated risks in publishing defamatory matter: the move to exact exemplary damages in the PQ 17 case serves to make this point. The argument is that only by punishing through damages, inflated to reflect disreputable conduct, can such publishers and authors be deterred from indulging their libellous pens. And even then to entitle the claimant to punitive damages it must be found that the miscreant deliberately calculated that the price would be worth paying in terms of enhanced circulation, and hence profits. I do not intend to digress into a discussion about the function of deterrence, suffice it to say, what deters whom, when and in what circumstances is a highly complex matter.

In ferreting out the ill deeds of evil-doers in our society, both politically and commercially, editors and publishers will (and do so now) weigh up the personal damage done to individuals in the wake of publication. But those that chuck their hats into the public arena – politicians, directors of public companies, and others who perform public services—cannot complain about the brickbats that are directed at them. They must learn to suffer the arrows of even outrageous criticism, because their occupation necessarily brings itself within the line of fire from a free Press. Moreover, quite the best way to find the truth is to allow comment to be disseminated unchecked, and to leave it to the reading public to determine where the truth lies. As the great judicial proponent of free speech, Mr Justice Holmes, said in *Abrams* v. *United States*[3] 'the best test of truth is the power of the thought to get itself accepted in the competition of the market'.

Yet if information and comment of public matters are to be allowed to go unbridled, there are three necessary steps to be taken to effect social control of scurrilous publications, to create the conditions necessary for there to be 'competition of the market', and to protect the individual in matters outside the purview of public interest.

A libel, as I have noted, is a crime. Slander, i.e., spoken defamation, is not in itself a crime, though in certain circumstances it may constitute a crime. The most notable, and modern example is the Race Relations Act 1965 which introduced the crime of incitement to racial hatred.

For some years now criminal prosecutions for libel have been rare, even to the point of falling into desuetude.* In one sense a prosecutor in a criminal trial has a less onerous burden to discharge than has the plaintiff in a civil action for libel,

* In *Regina* v. *Leigh* (17 March 1971) the accused, a property dealer, was convicted at the Old Bailey for publishing a 'defamatory libel' on a detective-sergeant, and was sentenced to six months' imprisonment to run consecutively with a sentence of five years imposed in November 1970 for fraud.

but that fact has not encouraged the use of the power to prosecute. Whereas in civil proceedings there must be a publication to a third party – a minor difference – and truth is a complete defence (only if proved), in a criminal prosecution publication to the person defamed is not enough and truth is not, by itself, any defence. Indeed, it is in the realm of criminal libel that the oft-cited dictum that 'the greater the truth, the greater the libel' has real meaning. Truth is no defence unless coupled with a plea that the publication was for the public benefit.

The most notable example in our legal history of a prosecution was when in 1895 Lord Queensberry stood in the dock at the Central Criminal Court charged with publishing a criminal libel on Oscar Wilde, calling him a homosexual. Lord Queensberry's acquittal became Wilde's subsequent conviction for having indulged in homosexual practices with consenting male adults in private, an offence happily consigned to the criminal history museum by Section 1 of the Sexual Offences Act 1967.

The publication of a libel is a criminal offence because it is an act calculated to provoke a breach of the peace. And there is no reason why a libel should not be the subject of a successful prosecution. A prosecution would obviously not ensue upon a libel of a trivial character. But is there any reason to withhold the criminal process where the libel is a particularly scandalous one and is being persisted in? Although the basis of the criminal offence is a provocation of a breach of the peace, it is no part of the duty of the prosecution to prove that in the circumstances of the case the libel was calculated to, or likely to, provoke such breach. And it is worth remembering that the publication of a defamatory libel upon a dead person will amount to a criminal offence, if it is of such a character as to injure the deceased's reputation in posterity. There is no such concern by the civil law for the wounded feelings of the deceased's family.

It is also a crime to publish a libel upon a body of persons, even though no individual is referred to by name or otherwise identified – provided that such libel is calculated to excite a breach of the peace, either by retaliation from members of a class, or by reason of the high feeling which it stimulates among other persons against the class. This dead letter of the law has received some indirect revival by the extension of the criminal law to incitement to racial hatred – a recognition of the public willingness to invoke criminal sanctions against the pedlars of literature and purveyors of language which are inimical to racial harmony. This provision in the Race Relations Act 1965 has not been an unqualified success: the culprits of the spread of the more virulent forms of racialism manage always to wrap their verbal wares in a parcel of respectability ('Some of my best friends are Jews' is the classic plea of the rabid anti-semite – including some Jews!). But at least this statutory development argues tellingly in favour of greater use of the weapon of criminal libel prosecutions.

It is not to be expected – nor to be advocated – that resort to criminal prosecutions would be common. Indeed it might be that proceedings would be largely confined to cases where it is necessary to intervene to protect persons in the discharge of public or judicial duties. An example where it was so used occurred in Australia in January 1960 when the publishers and editor-in-chief of the *Adelaide News* were charged with criminal libel. The charges arose out of the publication of posters and headlines making allegations against members of a Royal Commission investigating the case of a part-Aborigine convicted of murder in the Supreme Court of South Australia; the members of the Royal Commission included the Chief Justice of South Australia.

Such prosecutions, some would argue, might be invoked to protect political tyranny and bureaucratic corruption. But the instrument of criminal prosecutions is a risky weapon when encountering an independent judicial system, and may boomerang on those who wield it. And it is Parliament's function to be vigilant over misuse of the power of prosecution.

This criminal law offence is not to be confused with the respective crimes of publishing a blasphemous, seditious or obscene libel. Blasphemous libel – the use of language having a tendency to vilify the Christian religion or the Bible – is obsolescent, if not obsolete.* Seditious libel is a rarity. The

* A private prosecution was launched by Lady Birdwood against the directors of *Council of Love*, which ran for two months at the Criterion Theatre in 1970 (see *Guardian*, 18 February 1971, p. 11), but the summons was withdrawn at the hearing on 18 February 1971 (see ibid., 19 February 1971, p. 5).

most notable and unpropitious case in modern times was the unsuccessful prosecution – in 1947 – of Mr James Caunt, the editor of the *Morecambe and Heysham Visitor* when he wrote editorially at the time of the Stern gang's activities in Palestine that 'if British Jewry is today suffering from the righteous wrath of British citizens then they have only themselves to blame for their passive inactivity. Violence may be the only way of bringing them to a sense of their responsibility to the country in which they live.' (The prosecution could hardly have failed if the Race Relations Act 1965 had been in force.)

Prosecution for obscene libel is far from being a dead letter. It is in fact a constant threat not only to purveyors of pornography but also to the publishers of works of serious literature, although their vulnerability, exposed in a series of prosecutions in the late 1950s, has been mitigated by the special defence of public good under Section 4 of the Obscene Publications Act 1959.

If society desires to control the flow of obscene publications solely by the instrument of the criminal law, there is reason to suppose that it is willing similarly to suppress (or try to suppress) scurrilous libels which are not obscene but which the authorities consider offend against the public good. The sense of responsibility of editors and publishers will be the more nearly induced by the controlled threat of penal sanctions than it will be by the arbitrary use of the individual's right to proceed for damages in the civil courts. If the prosecutions against the publishers of *Lady Chatterley's Lover* and of *Last Exit to Brooklyn* do not induce confidence in the wise use of the power to prosecute, the verdicts of the courts in both cases – a jury acquittal and a quashed verdict on appeal respectively – will induce caution in the Director of Public Prosecutions, who is the sole arbiter of prosecution policy in this area of the criminal law.

The comparatively cumbrous method of criminal prosecution, since it requires sparing use, needs to be bolstered by a further revision in the law to permit publication to be matched by counter-publication. The battle of words is at present unevenly waged. The publisher has at his disposal – this is particularly true of the press – a more pervasive and readily available medium to propagate the written word. The individual person needs to be put into a position where the same breadth of dissemination for his views is available to counteract inaccurate information. The iniquity about journalistic untruths is that, by and large, they go unchallenged, and in consequence the words impress themselves upon the public mind. If the victim of defamatory matter were entitled to equal space and prominence in the same publication, the reader would be in a position to choose between evenly competing voices.

The Press Council in its informal way, upon a complaint being validated, does impose upon the relevant newspaper the duty of correcting the wrong perpetrated. But this limited power needs to be strengthened, and probably by statutory provision. There are two distinct aspects to this problem. One is that anyone attacked publicly should have the right of reply, perhaps statutorily provided, quite apart from the fact whether or not he has been libelled. The letter-to-the-editor columns already perform this but the right to reply is too often arbitrarily denied. The Press Council needs the power to demand on behalf of the individual that the right is accorded, irrespective of the merits of the dispute or the subject matter.

The second aspect, which is more relevant to the immediate problem of defamation, is the right of the individual to have any complaint investigated. If the individual is dissatisfied simply with the exercise of the right to reply, he should have the opportunity of complaining to an investigatory body (the Press Council) which, if it found the complaint substantiated, should have the power to order both publication of its findings and, where necessary, an apology in adequate terms. This function is already performed by a Press Council without any power to order publication of a finding in favour of the complainant.[4]

All these proposals would operate in the public domain. In the area of private interest, the individual's personal life should remain inviolate from publication. He is entitled not to have his character publicly besmirched, even if the publisher can establish the truth of his publication. It is a defect in the present law of libel, in my view, that a publisher can say anything about a person so long as he can prove it is true. There seems to be no morality in such a state of the law. If a retired Colonial Governor leaves his wife and goes to live in the West Indies with his paramour (as was once headlined in a popular newspaper) it is nothing to the journalist's credit that he can prove his story up to the hilt. The ex-Governor and his lady-love were entitled to immunity from public exposure. This in essence is what is involved in the right of privacy.

It is claimed by the detractors of the proposals for a new legal remedy for invasion of privacy that it is not possible to define, with the necessary degree of legal precision, what is and what is not a matter of public interest. Publishing the facts about the private sexual activities of a Minister of the Crown would not be a matter of public interest such as to confer any immunity on the publisher from an action for invasion of privacy. But if a Minister gets abusively drunk at an official reception, the reporting of such a happening would be a matter of public interest. In any event, newspapers (at least the serious ones) are constantly having to make decisions about 'publishability' on just these lines. And if even the truth of matters pertaining to individual privacy would no longer be publishable for fear of a lawsuit, perhaps the less serious newspapers would be driven to paying greater regard to what goes into their papers. That would ring the death knell of gossip-columns, which would be no bad thing.

Courts, moreover, should not find it impossibly difficult to decide where to draw the line, however jagged it might become as a result of case-law. A tentative step towards delineating the boundary line between public and private matter was made by Mr Justice Ungoed-Thomas in *Argyll* v. *Argyll*.[5] There the judge held that the marital relationship demanded protection for private communications between husband and wife so as to stop the *People* from publishing in that paper a weekly series on the private life of the Duchess of Argyll. The injunction granted by the court was in effect an action for the invasion of privacy.

On the reverse side of the coin, a right of an ex-employee to communicate confidential information of great public moment to the Press was upheld by the Court of Appeal in *Initial Services Ltd* v. *Putterill*.[6] There, a former employee of a firm of launderers supplying towels for use in machines handed information to the *Daily Mail* indicating restrictive practices in the laundry business, contrary to the Restrictive Trade Practices Act 1956. When sued for the delivery up of confidential papers and for an injunction to restrain further communication to the Press, the ex-employee pleaded that the employer's right to impose an obligation on a servant (or former servant) not to disclose information or documents received in confidence could not extend to any business practice which in the public interest ought to be publicly known and discussed. The Court declined to accede to the laundry firm's request to strike out the defence on the ground that it disclosed no defence known to the law. Far from acceding to the request to drive the ex-employee from the judgment seat, the Court went so far as to say that the defence had a reasonable prospect of success – a modern recognition of the citizen's overriding duty to expose public misconduct or maladministration, and a corresponding right in the Press to receive and publish matters of public interest.

Supposing the ex-employee's communication to the Press (and its subsequent communication) had contained defamatory matter, it might be that the publisher could have pleaded justification or fair comment on a matter of public interest. But until that issue was tried, the publisher might have been restrained either by injunction or the *sub judice* rule from continuing to publish the defamatory matter and other related information. It is my thesis that such nice questions should not arise, but that the publication is in the public interest and should remain untrammelled by the effect of the civil libel laws.

The demarcation between private and public matters is in any event an essential ingredient of any new 'right of privacy' law. Most of the legislative attempts to establish a new legal remedy have started from assumptions that there should be a right of action to anybody whose personal affairs or conduct were related by any form of mass media communication without the person's consent. Such proposals further envisage three defences: (a) if the publisher genuinely did not intend to refer to the individual suffering from the relaying of the information; (b) if the occasion was privileged, e.g. a report of parliamentary or judicial proceedings; and (c) where both the individual and the published matter were subjects of reasonable public interest; it is at this point that any such new right coalesces with the above-proposed reforms of the libel laws.

The great benefit to be derived from this substituted form of civil action is that one gets out of the hatred-ridicule-and-contempt syndrome. It is enough if the individual's personal life has been intruded upon. It depends on a factual situation, and not on a jury's or judge's opinion whether the language is defamatory. Furthermore, the inviolability of private life could not be penetrated on the ground that what was revealed was simply the unvarnished truth.

A new right of action for the invasion of privacy would set the seal on a fundamental principle of the citizen's right to be left in peace. English law has always recognized, with a commendable degree of fondness, that an Englishman's home is his castle, impregnable even to the police in execution of their duty, unless armed with a warrant. While the courts have firmly bolted the front door, even to constituted authority, they seem to have countenanced access through the back door to the idle and prurient curiosity of those persons who act largely uncontrolled by the law. That route needs blocking. At the same time a concession needs to be made for governmental doors to be opened more widely to public scrutiny. The public assault on that section in the Official Secrets Act 1911 which puts a damper on the dissemination of *any* confidential information from public sources is a healthy sign that the public wants to know more of what is done in its name by public servants.

If the proposals outlined are enacted, the whole emphasis of the purveying of news would be changed: switched away from the material that fills the gossip columns to the matters for which individuals are publicly accountable. Only when the pendulum has swung away from private intrusion to disclosure of public issues will the organs of publication stake their claim along with the Press to be the Fourth Estate of the realm.[7]

References

1 [1971] 2 W.L.R. 853.

2 It was Sir Winston Churchill who said that the United States is a 'land of free speech. Nowhere is speech freer – not even here where we sedulously cultivate it even in its most repulsive form', 28 September 1944.

3 250 U.S. 216 (1919).

4 See H. Phillip Levy, *Press Council: History, Procedure and Cases*, Macmillan 1967.

5 [1967] Ch. 302.

6 [1968] 1 Q.B. 396.

7 'The gallery in which the reporters sit has become a Fourth Estate of the realm', Lord Macaulay, *On Hallam's Constitutional History*, 1828.

Three

Reading between the Lines – The Lawyers and the News Desk

Anthony Lincoln, Q.C.

I have never been a goalkeeper, but I should imagine that he suffers much the same sort of experience as the legal adviser to a national newspaper. He may spend a glorious afternoon saving one hard shot after another until his hands tingle. But the one inglorious moment when the ball sped past him into the net is the moment the crowd remembers, the moment his team find it hard to forgive. The saves are not recorded; the misses are chalked up for all to see.

The newspaper lawyer longs to tell his editor of that low dive with which he brilliantly saved a fast, curving libel from getting into the paper. But if at the time the editor has his hands full with a heavy libel action which could end in an award of a princely sum against his newspaper, he will tend to be preoccupied with the libel that got through, not the one that was scotched.

Not that the newspaper lawyer has any right to be sorry for himself. He is in an enviable position. He is stationed at a strategic point which enables him to see, as it is happening, the impact of our much criticized law of libel on the written word. He can see how the law works 'in the field'. He can mitigate some of its hardships for the journalists. He can help them in some cases by a periphrasis here, a dodge there, to evade its less desirable restrictions and to get their message across to their readers, a little mutilated perhaps but still alive and kicking.

Above all it is very satisfying for newspaper lawyers to be in attendance during the actual process of putting a newspaper together. Many of them are practising barristers who are more accustomed to giving advice as counsel when the wrong has already been committed and the moment for preventive medicine has passed. All too often their role as consultants is confined to picking up the broken pieces after the deed is done and dealing as best they can with the consequences.

Sitting at the editorial or news desk, the libel lawyer is admirably placed to see the journalist as both perpetrator and victim of wrongs. Indeed the job requires an imaginative double-vision lawyer. He has to look at every passage, every phrase with the eye of the reader who picks up the paper at breakfast and sees that the passage is about *him*. How will that reader feel? Will he be so incensed as to take the immeasurable step of seeing his lawyer, and if he does, will he plunge into a law suit? Or on the contrary will he take the view that any publicity is good publicity?

At the same time the libel lawyer has to consider the driving need of every newspaperman to tell a good story, to be lively. Safety is not the objective of competent libel-reading. It is the work of a moment to render a passage harmless, guaranteed libel-free by removing every barb, every colourful allusion, every name from its contents. In doing so the lawyer may secure his goal-free record; but in the process he will have killed many a good piece of journalism stone dead.

It simply will not work for the legal adviser to aim at 100 per cent safety. And since he is not isolated from the people who bring the paper into existence (as he certainly would be if he were giving counsel from his usual lofty eyrie in the Temple), he comes to share the common appetite for risk and excitement. He knows that if the rival newspaper prints a good story which his own editor killed (acting on his advice that it was libellous), he will have to explain why. In fact, of course, there will often be a perfectly good explanation: it may be that the *Daily X* published the story, knowing full well that it was libellous, and deliberately took the risk of a libel action as an act of policy, whereas the *Daily Y*, having shelled out heavy damages in the previous six months, has decided that no risk is worth taking and that so far as libel risk goes, the paper is resting.

It may be, on the other hand, that the reporters of the *Daily X* have done more research on the story than those of the *Daily Y*. So they can put before their lawyers some useful corroborative evidence that the account they have given is true. The lawyer of *Daily Y* has no such comfort; he only knows the bare story and if it is untrue, his newspaper is defenceless. Can he trust his reporter or should he ask for more evidence than the reporter has produced?

Let us suppose that the story concerns a picture gallery the owner of which is reputed to be dealing in forged paintings. Nothing could be more defamatory than that. Now the libel lawyer is disturbed by this. For here is a good story which, if it be true, ought to be told and the public ought to be warned. But if it be false, a reputable dealer may find his reputation destroyed without the smallest justification. He will rightly sue the newspaper for damages and a sympathetic jury will not be allowed to forget that a single issue of the *Daily Y* can undo the work of a lifetime in building up a reputation.

This type of story serves as an excellent example for testing whether our libel laws are unduly oppressive towards the Press or properly protective of Everyman's hardly won and precariously secured reputation. Most defamatory pieces of journalism have no other *raison d'être* than the momentary delectation of a half-attentive reader; the libel is the seasoning for a jaded taste. But this sort of story, if true, ought to be published not only because it is good journalism but also for obvious moral reasons. So if the law of libel prevents its publication, there appears at first sight to be a case for saying that the law is in this regard defective. Let us see whether this case can be made out.

Theoretically if the story is true, then even though it is a defamatory story, the picture dealer cannot recover damages. He cannot obtain compensation to repair a reputation which deserved to be in disrepair. To state an elementary proposition of the law of libel, truth is a defence (and even journalists tend to believe in the contrary myth, 'the greater the truth, the greater the libel'). But theory and practice are poles apart. The story may be true but the newspaper if sued has to show a jury that it is true. The newspaper will have to call witnesses to say that the dealer sold paintings which were forged.

Now in an age when people do not wish to be involved, the willingness of the reporter's source to denigrate the picture is usually equalled by that source's reluctance to give evidence in a court of law. And worse still those who prove exceptions to the general rule by offering themselves as witnesses do so from motives which cast doubt on their accuracy. They may be envious competitors; they may have axes to grind. For this very reason they prove to be broken reeds in the witness box where enthusiasm, whatever its motivation, is less important than credibility.

Let us now return to the news desk of the *Daily Y* where the libel lawyer is chewing over his picture dealer story. There are probably only a few hours to go before the page carrying this story is to be set up in print. He has no doubt that it is libellous. He cannot defuse it, by removing, for example, the name of the picture dealer, for this would not only kill the piece for journalistic purposes; it would defeat the moral purpose which alone can justify the libel risk.

He cannot soften the impact of the story in any way by artful devices or hints. He therefore asks the reporter about his sources, their number, their reliability. The lawyer cannot assess their reliability. He must rely on the reporter; if he has worked on the paper for a period, he will have come to his own private conclusion as to which are the reliable ones, good at assessing the value of their own sources, which are the writers who fight tooth and nail for their own articles as if they were holy writ, without regard to the danger to which they are exposing not only their paper but also – and this tends to be forgotten – themselves personally.

No reporter likes to admit that he received his information at third hand. If it is, then the danger of error is doubled. Much riskier than all this is the 'scissor-and-paste' element. Many articles are compounded of fresh material direct from the horse's mouth, indirect material from the horse's stable lad, and cuttings from other newspapers which have already published something relevant to the article. In this way a piece of information which may or may not be accurate takes on the appearance of hard fact as it reappears in one publication after another; and this is simply because vigilant journalists rightly watch each other's writings for anything of value and engraft it on their own work. In journalism a mouse can in this way often give birth to a mountain of so-called fact, as was demonstrated in somewhat dramatic fashion by the Press at the Vassall inquiry. If false information is not killed by denial while in its infancy, it may grow into hard fact and enjoy great longevity.

But even apart from third-hand information, a sound piece of valid fact and comment founded on good sources carries its own inherent risk. Will the sources stand by what they have said if the picture dealer goes to his solicitor and threatens a law suit? Will they come to court? Of course, they can be compelled to do so by subpoena, but methods of compulsion are not always conducive to favourable evidence, specially if the reluctant witness finds himself engulfed in a long court case and forced to neglect his business. All this and much besides the lawyer has to weigh up before he can decide whether to advise his paper that the anti-forgery crusade should be called off before it becomes too expensive.

Does this impose too great a burden on the Press? Does it deter the Press from proper investigation and from the disclosure of scandals and wicked doings where disclosure can only be in the public interest? Before we consider the traditional retort of those who, like Cecil King, feel that the law hampers a freely inquisitive Press, let us complete the picture by seeing the publication of the story behind the story through the eyes of the picture dealer.

It has to be kept carefully in mind that neither the lawyer nor the reporter at the news desk of his paper *knows* that the dealer is in fact dealing in forged paintings. The reporter knows that the dealer has picked up a reputation for doing so, but that may well be because other dealers have maliciously created one for him. Neither the lawyer nor the reporter know that the dealer does this sort of thing, in the sense that they can be sure there is no innocent explanation for his actions and that they can persuade a jury there is none.

Let it be supposed that the picture dealer in question has on two occasions bought and sold a Leonardo da Botticelli (a pseudonym used only because habits of cautiousness die hard and even writing about the law of libel makes people jumpy). The two pictures turn out to be forgeries. But on each occasion he took advice from an eminent expert whose views on this non-existent painter are treated with great but not universal respect (for that is the way with experts). The advice was that on balance he considered the pictures genuine. So the dealer sold the pictures for a sizable sum. Then a few years later X-rays disclose overpainting which proves beyond doubt that the expert had nodded, the paintings were fake, the signatures forged.

The dealer, recognizing that in no time he will be risking his position in the art world, changes experts. But he is too late. The poison has started to spread and behind-the-hand accusations are made as to his integrity. A little of the poison reaches our reporter; he makes careful inquiries which disclose that the dealer is poorly thought of, but which do not disclose that the dealer took expert advice which led to his downfall.

The libel lawyer will of course ask the reporter if he has seen the dealer for his explanation; a question which any experienced reporter would rightly resent. The first thing he did was to speak to the man he was writing about. But as it turns out, that did not help. For the dealer, thrown into some agitation by the presence of the Press (a reporter's notebook is at least as frightening as a judge's wig), fails to mention that he had consulted an expert and had been advised that the pictures were genuine. This piece of the story thus never gets into the final article. But it is all-important, for it enables the fair-minded reader to judge for himself whether the dealer has behaved scandalously or is absolved from all blame.

Nobody in the foregoing is particularly to blame. In a court of law the dealer would have his own lawyers who would make a point of bringing out the significant and exculpating fact. The reporter did not know of it and the dealer forgot in his anxiety. The final story is damaging in the extreme and serves to publish to a circulation of a million people what before was unjustifiably believed by a handful in the art world.

And yet on the face of it this was a story which in journalistic terms scores heavily on all points. Art is news. There are scandals, not all of which find their way to court. The newspapers can uncover some which may otherwise go unpunished. But in doing so they may do untold damage to the innocent.

It is evident that both the libel lawyer and the reporter are concerned to ensure, within the limits of their situation, that the facts are right. These limits are severe. There is not much time to conduct an investigation on the lines of a criminal inquiry or a law suit. The spectre of obsolescence stalks noisily down Fleet Street and the suggestion that an article be deferred for further probing is not always received with acclamation. There is not much man-power; one reporter cannot spend his whole time on a story that may turn out to be no story at all, the 'scandal' that careful inquiry shows to be an innocent fact. Nor has the reporter the powers of a solicitor taking a statement from a potential witness or a detective gathering evidence for a criminal trial.

The high demands of accuracy are thus seen to be greatly inhibiting, and in many cases frauds who cannot be shown to be so are apt to get away with it, especially if they are trigger-happy about law suits. Recognizing this difficulty Mr Harold Lever, M.P. made an interesting proposal many years ago in an article he wrote for the *New Statesman.* He was largely responsible for piloting the Defamation Act 1952 through Parliament, a statute which alleviated the liability of newspapers in many undramatic ways. The proposal was solely concerned with the amount of damages awarded against newspapers for defamatory reporting. Briefly, Mr Lever's suggestion was that newspapers should be allowed to show how they came to make their fatal error. If they were to show that it was an honest mistake made after thorough inquiry, the damages payable would be mitigated by such conduct. 'Careless, callous reporting would still be heavily punished. Honest journalism would escape the worst.'

But would the Press not regard this as too high a price to pay for keeping down the damages? The sacred rule that journalists must never disclose their sources would have to be thrown to the winds. Not only would the reporter be required to tell the jury whom he questioned but what questions he asked, all to show how thorough were his inquiries. Even in these straitened times Fleet Street would opt for heavy damages rather than reveal to the world and rivals the inner workings of their reporting and editorial staff.

Frustrated in their efforts to unveil scandals and winkle out frauds, some newspaper proprietors have asked why there should not be a category of privilege which will protect a paper from libel suits where it publishes defamatory matter even if it turns out to be untrue. It is urged that provided the publication is not actuated by malice and provided that the material has been carefully compiled and honestly written, the publisher should not be liable to pay damages.

This rule, if it were adopted, would enable the reporter in the example I have given above to publish his article, leaving the picture dealer with no redress (except perhaps a correction in the paper which in practice is little consolation to the victim and irksome to editors). It would certainly encourage the pursuit and unmasking of scandals and free the Press from the need to look over its shoulder at unpredictable juries.

There are some lawyers who believe that this rule already exists in embryo form. In *Webb* v. *The Times Publishing Co. Ltd*, Mr Justice Pearson (now a Law Lord) gave a judgment in 1960 which was concerned with a newspaper report of foreign judicial proceedings. A newspaper is protected by statute in its reporting of English law suits. The question arose whether some similar protection arises in the reporting of foreign proceedings. Was the newspaper protected (even in publishing inaccuracies) by qualified privilege in this regard? In the circumstances of that case the judge decided that there was such protection. But some of his pronouncements have been interpreted to be of wider application. In one well-known passage the judge said:

> Could there be a plea of 'fair information on a matter of public interest' which would be coordinate with the familiar plea of 'fair comment on a matter of public interest'? The need for something like this arises because . . . privilege is required if there is to be any effective protection of a newspaper publishing reports of judicial proceedings when such reports are of public interest. In my view there not only ought to be, but there is such privilege.

From this position it is but a short stride to the wider one. If foreign law suits are of public interest, so are other events. Therefore, to quote the cautious words in the headnote of the law report on this case, it looks as though 'qualified privilege attaches to fair information on a matter of public interest'. So it is argued; and it should be added that Mr Justice Pearson defined public interest as 'legitimate and proper interest as opposed to idle curiosity or a desire for gossip'.

Nothing has occurred since 1960 to suggest that the embryo has grown into an adult rule giving newspapers any protection wider than simply reporting foreign proceedings. For it was this special class of event with which the judge was concerned and not *any* event of public interest. There has been no decision since *Webb* v. *The Times* incorporating the rule in its wider application; such a decision could have momentous consequences in terms of the freedom of the Press to investigate.

For it is the words 'public interest' that contain the possibility of great extensions of privilege. What is legitimate interest as opposed to idle curiosity or a desire for gossip? On the one hand the picture dealer's reputation could be said to be a matter for gossip among other dealers. His 'misconduct' affected only a handful of the million readers who read the article. On the other hand, *nil humanum a me alienum.* If anyone misbehaves in the market place, we should all hear about it. This concept of public interest raises many problems. It is not enough that the material is a matter of public news. The public may take the widest interest in a matter that is essentially private.

Libel lawyers are frequently faced with problems in this area of the law which are not capable of any hard and fast solution. Take the conduct of a politician. How far into his private life should a newspaper permissibly probe on the basis that it is a matter of public interest? There are those who take the view that politicians should be treated like actors. On-stage they invite criticism, they choose to expose their behaviour to the public and must take the brickbats with the bouquets. But off-stage they return to share the privileges of privacy with every other citizen; the limelights are doused.

There is a similar dichotomy in the life of a politician. He too has a private and a public life. Should the one be protected from the glare to which the other is exposed? One difficulty is that many politicians use their private lives as part of the leverage for their public reputation so that the two become entangled. In this case a newspaper can rightly claim to comment on all aspects of the man's behaviour at home or in the forum. But even where this is not the case, problems arise where a politician's private behaviour affects his public conduct of affairs. Excessive drinking in private may damage his political judgment. It may lead to an undiplomatic scene which damages the national interest. Private habits can lead to public disasters. Does this give the journalist a charter to write defamatory comments on an M.P.'s domestic life and claim that he was writing on a matter of public interest in the technical sense?

There is no answer which can give a logical solution. The case for the roving investigation is that it is in the public interest to warn the public of the possibility of disasters before they occur, rather than merely recording the obsequies. On this view the journalist has at the moment an impossible task. He takes the risk that if he gets his facts wrong, and if he cannot show that X's home life is a matter of public interest because it may have consequences in the political domain, he has landed his newspaper and himself in trouble.

The case against extended protection for probing the private sector of public men is simply stated: the journalist is first and foremost in pursuit of entertaining stories, and the heat of the pursuit is not conducive to the cool assessment of public interest in the limited sense in which we are using the concept. So what does the libel lawyer advise in such situations? In practice politicians are regarded as fair game for free and widely ranging comment. They do and should take the rough with the smooth. Without the newspapers they have no reputations; with them their reputations are at risk. Any politician who, taking advantage of the present ill-defined concept of public interest, rushed to his solicitors when he thought his private life improperly invaded, would find little sympathy with the jury or the British public of whom they are a cross-section.

If we now return, with these doubts in our mind as to the concept of public interest, to the picture dealer case, the libel lawyer will take risks in the interests of an exciting publication. But he cannot risk assuming that a critical article about the picture dealer can shelter behind the defence that it was 'fair information on a matter of public interest'. He will help the reporter to test the strength of the evidence and suggest potential sources of information which have been left untapped. He will do his best to save the article from being killed.

Despite such first-aid activities the final product may still contain a high risk element. Perhaps it would be better to omit the identity of the picture dealer. True, he can be identified by those in the know who can draw on their own knowledge from various indications in the text of the story. There may be only two dealers who handle Leonardo da Botticellis in England. Both could theoretically sue. He must weigh up whether it is likely that they would emerge from their relative obscurity and identify themselves by starting a law suit, thus increasing the number of people in the know from a handful to the million who may read the proceedings; or whether their reputation in the eyes of their few colleagues matters so much to them that they will prefer the vindication of a law suit.

The final decision lies not with the reporter or the lawyer but with the editor and proprietor who in the end are liable to pay the damages if any. The assessment of risk is the most important of the functions of the libel lawyer and the most difficult. Yet in practice, although the law of libel is vague and in many respects requires more restraint from the press than the latter can exercise without abdicating its function, advice and guidance can be given within its framework – not with certainty (it rarely can in other branches of law) but with a degree of objective assessment.

The present law requires the Press to live dangerously. But that is inherent in the business of producing news sheets. The libel lawyer is the doctor in the pits at Silverstone; the men he is caring for are there to drive dangerously. And the law is not altogether unhelpful to the press. The present Master of the Rolls, Lord Denning, has asserted many times in the Court of Appeal the importance of protecting a free Press from an over-oppressive law of libel.

Thus it is that the courts never issue injunctions to stop a newspaper from repeating a libel if the newspaper intends at the trial to prove the truth of the libellous statement. This can be very damaging to the victim. He is not interested in the ultimate trial of his action two or three years later. He is interested to stop the libel tomorrow in case it does him irreparable damage. It is little consolation to him that he will get heavier damages in the long run. There may never be a long run.

This is a salutary rule and one that should be thrown into the balance when the Press fret at their inability to be ombudsmen without risk. The Press, guided by their lawyers, are inevitably tight-rope walking when they probe scandals. Under the existing law it is dangerous but not impossible. It merely calls for skill and a cool head. If government and bureaucracy become oppressive, there is no problem. Civil servants cannot or do not sue, nor do administrators. It is the private tyrants in industry, trade and the professions who have to be watched carefully. They need their court jesters more than any Lear did. Perhaps we need a licensed jester newspaper wholly privileged to utter the most libellous statements about our latter-day kings and so cut them down to size. *Private Eye* would be a useful start. But who would issue the licences?

Four

Libel – A Book Publisher's View

William Kimber

Some years ago I was studying the affairs of a small publishing company that had run into financial difficulties, and one of the nails in its coffin was a liability it had incurred for £2,000 in settlement of a libel claim. The total cost was more than £2,000 because there was the considerable residue of the edition of the novel and the legal expenses. Say the total was about £3,000 and taking into account that this incident was in the late 1940s it represents the sort of figure which was quite enough to be a serious blow to a private firm whose resources were already strained. And these were the circumstances: the complaint had been made about a novel by a prolific author, and the publishers had no reason to suppose that it was other than entirely fictitious throughout. But some time before writing this novel the author had made accusations about an official in the locality in which he lived, and these accusations had led to a libel action by the official against the author and the official had won. In the novel the author had introduced a character who was clearly identifiable as the official and had portrayed him committing the misdeeds about which he had already brought a successful action against the author. The publishers had known nothing about this earlier episode, and had no reason to suspect the author of any libellous disposition. Indeed, many of his novels had been published by a group of publishers for which I had worked, and none of them had produced any legal trouble. In view of the earlier proceedings, of which they had known nothing, the unfortunate firm had no alternative but to settle and, so they told me, they had been unable to recover the money from the author. This is an example of publishers suffering the consequences of a libel of which they are themselves morally innocent but for which they are liable in law.

Measures were introduced into the Defamation Act of 1952 to reduce the liability of authors and publishers arising from innocent libel. These measures would have been of no avail to the publishers in the case I have outlined, because they were not innocent in the eyes of the law. Two essential elements were missing without which the 1952 Act gives the publishers no mitigation. One is that it would not have been possible to rebut the claim that the character was identifiable as the plaintiff, and the other is that the publishers would have been unable to prove, as the Act makes incumbent upon them if they are asserting innocence, that the author wrote without malice.

Even where the definition of innocent libel can be shown to be fulfilled, the procedure of 'making amends' can be expensive; for it entails withdrawing the book from sale, making a public apology and following a strict legal procedure for which the publisher has to pay the plaintiff's costs as well as his own. If the withdrawal from circulation of a book occurs shortly after publication, at the same time that it is likely to be reviewed, the delay that occurs before it can be available in the book shops again jeopardizes its prospects of selling. For unless demand can be met immediately a book tends to get forgotten by the public who in the meanwhile will have had plenty of other new books paraded to them by reviewers and booksellers. If only one page has to be replaced to remove offending passages, that one new page has first to be printed, the original page removed and the new page 'tipped in' by the binders. Allowing for the time taken for the books to be returned to the publishers from the booksellers, followed by the publishers sending all their remaining stock to the binders and then the distribution process all over again, a delay of at least some weeks is inevitable. By losing the market for the book the publisher may be left with such a substantial proportion of his edition unsold that the financial effect, particularly if the edition was a large one, is equivalent to paying damages.

Such, as things stand, can be the cost of 'innocent libel' where the plaintiff has agreed to an offer of amends. For the libel to qualify for such classification the publishers must show either that they did not intend to publish the words 'of and concerning' the person, and did not know of circumstances by virtue of which they might be understood to refer to him, or that the words were not defamatory on the face of them, and the publishers did not know of circumstances by virtue of which they might be understood to be defamatory of that person. Also the publishers must have 'exercised all reasonable care in relation to the publication'. Furthermore, and this is a condition likely to create profound difficulties to fufil, to take advantage of this section of the Act, the publishers must prove that the words were written by the author without malice.

The ameliorating provisions of the 1952 Act would likewise have been of no advantage in an instance given to me by Mr Hamish Hamilton. In a book called *Dinner at the White House* the author, Louis Adamic, had added to the final proofs, without telling the publishers, a footnote which was defamatory of the late Sir Winston Churchill and as a result of which Churchill was paid substantial damages. None of the conditions necessary to dispose of the matter by an offer of amends would have applied. In effect, it seems to me that the 'innocent' libel section of the Act can only very rarely be of use to book publishers, though its value to newspapers must be very great. If it were reported of Mr X that he was engaged to be married, but it turned out that he was already a married man and Mrs X brought a complaint, then an immediate offer of apology by the newspaper would make it inadvisable for her to proceed against them with a claim for damages. This is as it should be, but it was not so before 1952.

But accidental confusion arising from bald reporting of fact seldom occurs in the more detailed context of a book. If a book is alleged to be defamatory the publisher will almost certainly be sued simultaneously with the author, and if the action is defended by both of them if they lose and damages are awarded against them then the plaintiff is entitled to recover these damages from either defendant. In a recent libel action in the Queen's Bench Mr Justice Lawton, during legal argument about a plea for punitive damages and in the absence of the jury, vividly described the publisher's worst libel nightmare. I should emphasize that the judge was proposing a purely hypothetical situation for the purpose of legal argument and was not referring to any of the parties in the case. His remarks to counsel were:

> What is the position when there is really outrageous conduct on the part of the author, he hoodwinks the publishers into thinking that the book is a sound book, can be justified up to the hilt, and the publishers, believing him, publish and then it is found that the author was full of malice and was coldly calculating that worldwide publicity would be worth the risk of paying the sum of damages an English jury might feel inclined to award; can the publisher turn round and say that it does not apply to him because it is one judgment? It is a highly technical matter.

To which counsel replied: 'It is', and the discussion of this hypothesis proceeded no further. From this I infer that there is no ready-made answer in law to a situation such as Mr Justice Lawton postulated. If this is so, then some reform is surely called for whereby a publisher can avoid punishment or ruin if he can show that he acted carefully and in good faith.

The two examples that I have given are intended to illustrate the fact that as the law stands a publisher may suffer a heavy financial blow from causes of which he is, in the ordinary and natural meaning of the word, innocent, but not 'innocent' according to the application of that word to the law of libel. But this is not to deny that in most cases of libel within my experience a publisher must rely chiefly on two counsellors – his own common sense and his own conscience. After all, in stark outline, the English law is fairly clear. Any words capable of a defamatory meaning which refer to a living person can give rise to a libel action. And there are six defences: innocence (as technically defined); truth; fair comment on a matter of public interest; that the words do not refer to the plaintiff; that they do not have the meaning imputed to them or any meaning which is defamatory of the plaintiff; that they are 'privileged' (i.e. derive from court or parliamentary proceedings, and other special circumstances). The plaintiff has three aspects to prove; that the words have been published to a third person, that they are capable of a defamatory meaning and that they have been taken by reasonable people to refer to him. Within these simple boundaries lies a maze of complexities in which the finest brains of the English law often probe their way to quite opposite opinions. And as most libel actions are tried by a jury, it usually falls to the combined common sense and intelligence of twelve ordinary citizens to sort out and decide upon the tangled web that the lawyers have laid before them. A publisher may have as good a chance as anybody, including his lawyer, of guessing what a jury's reaction is going to be. And perhaps more than anyone else is he in a better position to assess the author's state of mind concerning the matter which has produced the alleged libel.

The complexity of libel stems from the intangibility of libel. Both sides, plaintiff and defendant, confront each other in court as a result of states of mind, except in special cases where the plaintiff has suffered some direct adverse practical consequence from the libel. But a state of mind is of course a major condition of life, and an injury to a state of mind may be as serious or more serious than an injury to physical health or to financial security. It is imperative that the law should give protection to those who have been psychologically distressed or suffered material loss through an untrue and damaging statement about them. When an author has written something which he believes to be true he naturally recoils from any formal and public statement to the contrary. It is on this question of truth that so often an author's pride is hurt when for the sake of expediency he is advised to compromise. In the course of discussing with a highly successful Queen's Counsel the possibility of his writing his memoirs in his retirement he kept coming back to the obstacle of libel. I said: 'But surely you of all people don't need to be advised about libel.' He replied, 'No, but I also know the difference between what I *know* to be true and what I can *prove* to be true.'

'The difference between what I *know* to be true and what I can *prove* to be true.' If this distinction were engraved on the pen of every writer who wrote about the living there would be fewer libel cases – there would also be fewer books.

Libel complaints can develop and in effect get out of hand because both plaintiff and author feel that their integrity has been impugned. And they can each reach a state of mind in which they are both, with equal integrity, entitled to that state of mind. As an illustration I recall a passage in a book by a racing driver which described an accident which cost many lives. The author described the accident as he faithfully recollected it, but the lawyer who vetted the manuscript for libel wanted, and obtained, confirmation from an independent motor racing expert that the description was in line with what was generally accepted as a correct account in motor-racing circles. Nevertheless, another driver who was mentioned in the passage felt that it imputed some blame to him and started libel proceedings. I know that what the author had written he honestly believed to be an accurate description and that he had not intended his words to be critical of the other driver, and that had the case come to trial he would have had many witnesses to support his account. Nevertheless, the accident must have occupied only a second or two in time, and a recollection of it some years later would inevitably vary from one person to another. Both men were doubtless equally sincere in their different recollections, but the clash would have led to the equivalent, in the form of a libel action, of a full-scale inquiry into the causes of the accident. The case did not come to trial as one of the drivers died while it was pending. I have mentioned it as representing the preponderance of the psychological element in libel, and how it can touch issues of deep personal significance against which financial considerations take second place.

Another source of psychological conflict is when a passage genuinely meant as a favourable reference or even a tribute is interpreted as hostile and libellous. As an example of this I recall an episode in a book about a German sea raider in which it was said of the captain of a victimized British merchant ship that he had successfully duped the German captain by deluding him into believing that all the British crew had been taken off the sinking merchantman. Instead, the book related, he had left behind the wireless operator, who to the discomfiture of the German captain sent signals from the sinking ship which alerted other vessels and the Royal Navy. Solicitors for the British captain complained that the passage was libellous because it showed him as betraying the tradition that he should be the last to leave a sinking ship and that it was untrue that he had done otherwise. No such criticism was implied in the context, in which the captain of the German raider, though endangered by what had happened, complimented the British captain for having successfully outwitted him. Nevertheless, the British seaman considered the story seriously libellous. I made inquiries among a number of senior naval officers, and the majority view was that what had been written of the captain was a creditable *ruse de guerre* and comparable to the Royal Navy's tradition of never surrendering but leaving aboard a scuttling party to sink the ship. There were some, however, who thought that the merchant navy might take a different view and could understand his complaint. The matter did not go beyond the preliminary stages because of the captain's death. I think it illustrates the hazards of even apparently favourable references to living persons being construed as defamatory, and bearing in mind the division of opinion I encountered among naval experts, no lawyer could reasonably have been expected to anticipate a dispute arising from this *prima facie* complimentary passage.

An even more startling example of unexpected complaint arrived from solicitors representing someone whose name had been included amongst those people mentioned and thanked by the author at the beginning of his book for having helped him while he was preparing it. This person's name was referred to with gratitude for having discussed with the author the subject of a particular chapter. The complaint arrived in our office a few days before the book was due for publication – the person mentioned having seen a review copy – and it alleged that this chapter of the book was so inaccurate that the mention of the person's name as a source of its information was damaging to him in his professional capacity. The solicitors asked for an undertaking that the book would not appear with their client's name left in it, and said that they would seek an immediate injunction from a judge in chambers unless we undertook to withdraw it. Luckily I was able quickly to get the chapter read by the most senior living authority on the subject, who not merely said he could find no fault with the material but described it as 'excellent'. The complaint was not pursued.

Someone who writes to a publisher claiming that a passage is defamatory and untrue is impugning the truthfulness of the author. It is an accusation which in its own way may be as damaging to the author as the passage in question may be to the accuser. For apart from the legal expenses that follow from dealing with libel complaints, the demands upon a publisher's time which they make can be a perilous diversion from the constructive activities of his work. And an author who gets a reputation for reckless statements may find his manuscripts receiving less enthusiastic welcome from potential publishers. An author once told me that he had seen on a newspaper editor's desk a memorandum from the proprietor referring to himself, the author, which read: 'In dealing with X you must be sure of his sources, otherwise he is not worth all the trouble.'

An author tends to repudiate a libel complaint, unless it relates to a plain question of fact on which it can be incontrovertibly shown that he has made a mistake. This is a natural reaction for it touches his personal qualities of truthfulness, conscientiousness and soundness of judgment and his material interest in his reputation. The publisher and the author may both be professionally advised that there is no adequate defence, and when this occurs there is nothing to be done except to negotiate the most reasonable terms of a settlement. But there are circumstances when the issue for the author and the issue for the publishers are widely apart in their degrees of importance. This can arise particularly when the author of the book is not a writer by profession but the alleged libel is one which, if he is guilty of it, would reflect gravely upon him in the sphere in which he may be professionally prominent, and equally when the subject-matter of the contested material affects a cause with which the author, but perhaps not the publishers, is closely concerned and in which some relatively simple solution such as an apology would gravely jeopardize the author's position against his special background.

I believe that it is one of the main duties of a publisher to help to keep an author out of the courts as a defendant in a libel action. Because even if a defendant wins and is awarded costs these are in practice less than his entire costs and do not include any compensation for the time he will have expended during the preparation and hearing of the case, and his losses through the withdrawal of the book from circulation while the trial was pending, if this frequent measure was taken. The danger of potential libel, and the handling of a complaint of libel, produce some of the most difficult and delicate aspects of publisher–author relationship. Setting aside for the moment a consideration of the usual indemnity clause in the publishing contract there can be a wide gulf, as I have just suggested, between the importance of a libel question to the author and to the publisher. One's sympathies tend to lie with the author who on some evidence believes that he is entitled to write something that might be considered defamatory of X because he has reached the conclusion that it is true and that it is a matter of contemporary history to publish it. Certainly if Gibbon's definition of history as a 'register of the crimes, follies and misfortunes of mankind' is accepted, then the English law of libel has a constrictive effect on current history. Because the essence of that law is that he who asserts must prove, and the proof required is proof up to the hilt,* and the author will fail if he can show only that the defamatory statement was true on the balance of probability based on the evidence before him. No matter with what degree of objectivity the author has reached a defamatory conclusion the rigour of the law in requiring proof is likely to lead the publisher's legal adviser to suggest its omission unless cast-iron proof is available. The chasm between balance of probabilities and proof of truth is such as can very easily give rise in an author's mind to the suspicion that his work is being subjected to personal censorship under the guise of legal advice. It is a fact of human nature that cold objectivity and a talent for original and vivid writing seldom go hand in hand, and if an author approaches a subject with a passionate interest it is unlikely that he will be without a prejudice in one direction or another. He himself may be unaware of the prejudice, but the perspicacious publisher may recognize its existence and be aware of a tendency to give excessive credence to evidence of one sort while discounting equal evidence which may undermine his preconceived beliefs.

Discussing a lawyer's libel report with an author can be one of publishing's most delicate tasks. A great amount of research may lie behind the questioned passages, and if they reflect

* With the proviso that if the defamation consists of several allegations complete proof of the most serious of them is sufficient.

the author's considered distillation of sources it is naturally frustrating for him to be asked to jettison what he may regard as fresh and important interpretation; such passages often, in his view, offer the most valuable and original material without which the book would appear far less striking to the reviewers and the public. In a situation where an author wants to persist in the publication of defamatory matter the publisher must frequently bear the responsibility of taking a risk. But it is important to define the nature of this risk. Few publishers would deliberately publish something which they knew to be both defamatory and untrue, but what does one do when confronted with defamation which the author declares to be founded on truth? His sources may be verbal of which a memorandum was made by him, but the accuracy of which one cannot know for sure; they may be notes of documents no longer in his possession; records, from either verbal or written sources, may derive from a foreign language one does not understand. It is usually quite impracticable to check all source material to its ultimate origins, and even to try to do so implies a disbelief of the author's assurances. Professional advice will indicate the degree of seriousness of the allegation and the measure of evidence necessary if it is challenged, but where there is a gulf between what revisions or deletions the legal adviser suggests and what the author is prepared to do, then the publisher is faced with the unenviable choice of telling his author, in effect, that he distrusts his truthfulness or his judgment or of proceeding with material about which he has been warned. The risk lies in the publisher's assessment of the author's probity, and from his wider association with him he may be better placed to make a reliable assessment than the lawyer. Again, the publisher must ultimately resort to his conscience and his common sense.

Some authors are anxious to steer clear of litigation and are wholly co-operative in following the recommendations of a libel report. Some tend to burden one's credibility in their resourcefulness in seeking to justify every statement, and occasionally a report provokes virulent hostility. I have had a libel report drawn up by a Queen's Counsel described by the author as 'a form of masturbation by a Benedictine monk in heat' [*sic*]. It is difficult for some writers to understand a law in which a *bona fide* belief in the truth of a libellous statement is no defence and can, at best, avail only to mitigate damages.

The chairman of one of England's leading group of book publishers has told me how often he has been left 'holding the baby' after taking the precaution of suspending sales of a book after getting a libel complaint which appeared to have *prima facie* some substance, but about which he was unable to consult the author immediately through the latter's absence abroad. In several situations of this kind he has later found the author criticizing the precautionary measures and denying the alleged libel. Yet a publisher has to accept responsibility in law and possibly bear the entire financial burden of an adverse outcome. 'Who', this publisher pertinently asks, 'is the principal?'

Precedents in the courts have shown that when a publisher has taken no action following a complaint, and continued to sell the book, the damages have been thereby heavier. Instructing the trade department not to fulfil orders for a book until further notice is a compromise which, though it may sometimes be a crippling blow to the book's sales, is much less drastic than formally recalling all copies already in circulation, but it is a step which would be a mitigating factor for both author and publisher if the complaint proved serious.

A clause under which the author indemnifies the publishers against libel is a standard feature of publishing contracts. Its phraseology varies, and when the indemnity applies only to 'libel' as distinct from 'actions brought on the grounds that the work contains libellous matter' the paradoxical situation can arise that it is in the publisher's interests that an alleged libel should be admitted by the author or proved against him, for in such wordings it is only when the libel has been established that the indemnity can be invoked. This means that if the publisher assists the author to refute the alleged libel then he stands to lose from his efforts. The case of the doctor from Auschwitz, Dr Dering, who brought a libel action against the author of the novel *Exodus*, Mr Leon Uris, and my firm as the publishers, is mentioned elsewhere in this book (see p. 128). The first letter of complaint arrived in my office in April 1962. The phrase about the doctor was only a passing reference within a sentence, but the allegation was serious. A preliminary look at the official volumes of the Nuremberg Trials revealed that witnesses there had implicated him in their evidence concerning other people, but he himself had not been arraigned there and these allusions were too vague to serve as a defence. However, the Frankfurt War Crimes Prosecutor gave me a few leads, and one of these led to the list of between 150 and 200 witnesses who would have been called by the prosecution in the trial of Dr Clauberg who had been Dr Dering's German superior in the Auschwitz surgical experiments, and who had died in prison while awaiting trial in West Germany. This list, and other sources, was worked on from my office for some months with the result that a substantial core of evidence was obtained from victims and witnesses to point to the truth that at least a considerable number of experimental operations had been performed by Dr Dering. In October of that year Mr Uris came to London to decide whether the case should be defended or settled, and Lord Gardiner was consulted. Lord Gardiner was asked for his view on two counts; firstly, whether the action should be defended, and secondly, whether the indemnity clause was valid. His answer to the first was 'Yes' and I recall his adding that he thought it was a public duty to do so. His answer to the second was 'No', because there was evidence to show that the allegation was true and therefore not a libel.* Thus the evidence my firm had collected had invalidated the indemnity clause.

The Dering case also illustrates the divergence that *could* arise between publisher and author if one of them wished to take a position on a matter of principle and the other to dispose of a complaint with the minimum of trouble and financial risk. In this instance the problem did not arise for both Mr Uris and my firm wished to resist Dr Dering's claims for damages and an apology after we had seen the preliminary evidence of his Auschwitz activities, and an arrangement for the costs of the defence was drawn up between the solicitors for Mr Uris and my firm's solicitors under which agreed proportions were contributed by the two defendants. But the financial alternatives

* With all the respect due to a great advocate and a former Lord Chancellor, perhaps I should add that in private conversation a Queen's Counsel specializing in libel has told me that he would not have held the same view as Lord Gardiner on this point.

were substantially different. Dr Dering at first asked for damages of £7,000 (and a High Court apology), in case, as applies so often, the defendants would have preferred a negotiated settlement out of court to the risks and inevitable expense of defending the action. Later the suggested sum was reduced to £2,000 and this would have embraced settlement with the author, ourselves, the printers and the paperback publishers (proceedings had not been brought against the last, but the proposed settlement would have averted this contingency). So £500 from each party concerned with publication would have ended their liability, and in fact this course was taken by the printers whose £500 and public apology were given to Dr Dering before the trial. It was estimated that the costs of defending a lengthy hearing would be about £25,000 and of course this did not allow for the possibility of Dr Dering being awarded heavy damages and his costs. The trial resulted in Dr Dering being awarded a halfpenny damages and ordered to pay the defendants' costs, but he was able to pay only a very small proportion of them; my firm's share of the legal expenses came to about £6,000, more than ten times the amount it would have incurred in a unanimous settlement, or about three or four times more than it would have cost them to have made a separate settlement.

The Dering case is one in which the author and the publisher took the same view and accepted that the issue at stake had priority over financial expediency. But it is easy to imagine situations where this does not occur, and a publisher may be placed in a position of subtle conflict. He may feel that the author is precarious in his ability to prove the truth of the alleged libel, and that the author is in no position to meet a full indemnity against the outcome of a trial though wanting to embark on a defence. If the publisher makes an independent settlement including an apology he undermines the author's position morally if not technically. A High Court apology may be widely reported, and can hardly be likely to benefit the author's cause. An apology in a newspaper for an alleged libel which the author may subsequently be successful in defending may in itself be a libel on the author, as the case of *Tracy* v. *Kemsley Newspapers** established. So a libel complaint leading to a difference of attitude between author and publisher has

* *The Times*, 9 April 1954.

complex considerations. When the complaint is not of a nature that reflects a major issue of principle it is probably the publisher's duty to prevent feelings on both sides from running too high. A minor slip by an author can ferment a suspicion of deliberate falsification. Tactful correspondence at an early stage can avoid potential tension, and reduce the danger of mutual hostility aggravating a merely infelicitous reference into an allegation of malicious defamation. A cool and prudent approach by the publisher can save the author and himself from becoming engulfed in comparatively trivial matters developing into formal proceedings with all their demands on time and pocket.

This discussion would become too specialized if I were to attempt to quote all the variations in the phraseology of the indemnity clause as it appears in somewhat different forms from one publisher to another and from one literary agent to another. Let us assume that its purport is that the author guarantees to the publisher that the book contains no libellous matter and that he will keep the publisher financially indemnified against any claims of libel. In theory, then, the publisher can look to the author to reimburse him for all the consequences of a libel complaint except the loss of his time which it may inflict. In practice, the author may have no funds to meet the costs and potential damages of an action and in such a case the indemnity is useless to the publisher. For a plaintiff is entitled to bring, and usually does, a consolidated action against both defendants, and any costs or damages he may be awarded he can recover from either defendant. If a publisher goes into a case as a co-defendant with an author of slender means then he is virtually shouldering the entire financial responsibility. To what extent are indemnity clauses morally fair in practice? I have seen it argued that it is unreasonable for a publisher even to expect any indemnity because it is part of his function to refer the manuscript to his legal adviser and ensure that no libel gets published, that this is an area in which his experience coupled with the advice he should seek should leave the responsibility upon him. I cannot accept such an argument, because there can be so many aspects and sources for a book which can lie hidden from the publishers, let alone his legal advisers;

and the absence of an indemnity would unquestionably be unfair in the hypothetical situation posed by Mr Justice Lawton which I have already quoted.

It seems to me that in this question of indemnity there are degrees of moral obligation according to the circumstances. I think that a publisher should be prepared to accept the risk of innocent libel as an occupational hazard and share its consequences with the author. Almost unbelievable coincidences are possible that could lead to the stringent and costly procedure of 'making amends', or settling a claim. The long arm of genuine coincidence was brought home to me a few years ago when I published the memoirs of a former member of the Secret Intelligence Service. It was the first occasion of a member of that service being permitted to write about it, and after protracted negotiations with the authorities permission was granted provided that the author published the book under an assumed name. I suggested to the author that he used the name of the Hertfordshire village of Whitwell, and the book was published as *British Agent* by John Whitwell. A short time after it came out a real Mr John Whitwell called at my offices; there was no question of libel; he had been an officer in military intelligence and was interested to find out a little more about his namesake. But what if a novelist had hit upon this name for a British intelligence officer depicted as in the traitorous service of the Russians? If an 'innocent' libel situation had arisen then it would have been hard on the novelist to bear the entire brunt of the publishers' out-of-pocket expense. In contrast, where a novelist has used his book, as in the example I gave in the opening of this article, to present defamatory matter of thinly disguised real people of which the publisher had no knowledge the consequences should be met, I feel, entirely by the author. For unless the publisher employs private detectives to explore the author's private circle of acquaintances how can he do other than accept in good faith that all the characters in a novel are, if the author so assures him, fictitious?

In non-fiction works dealing with living persons the problems of respective responsibility can be complicated by reasons I have already explained. It is impracticable for a publisher to go over the entire ground of an author's researches, and if the author claims that a *prima facie* defamatory statement is founded upon truth and urges publication despite a warning that truth is essential, then again I feel that morally he is accepting, and should bear, full responsibility. Of course I am assuming that the publisher has adopted a serious approach to the questioned material and has not encouraged the author to take a chance. If an element of irresponsibility is connived at by the publisher then he should not expect to enforce an indemnity. But a publisher can be placed in an ugly dilemma if an author who is valuable to his list adamantly presses for the inclusion of material which he feels justified in writing, but about which the publisher, possibly supported or alerted by his legal adviser, may have serious reservations. Such a dilemma can lead to a complete break with an author even if he is likely to stand by his indemnity. There are certain issues about which the publisher's conscience may take command of the situation and prohibit him from publication even if he is assured of financial protection from the risk.

The ameliorating section of the Defamation Act of 1952 gives no protection to the publisher unless he can prove that the author wrote 'without malice'. As I understand it, 'malice' in English law refers to a state of mind, a condition of conscious or emotional hostility. It must be very rare, though of course not impossible, for both the author and the publisher to have been motivated by malice. A publisher could encourage an author to write falsely and maliciously about a living person, and if he were to do so he should be accountable for the consequences. In practice, however, malice is usually concealed by the author and denied if suggested. Even in 'innocent' libel the publisher has no safeguard from damages unless he can prove the author's state of mind, and how he could do this I cannot begin to imagine. And in a trial in which a deliberate hostility towards the plaintiff on the part of the author may emerge from the evidence, a jury may take account of such hostility in arriving at the amount of damages. In a consolidated action against author and publisher (as is almost inevitable) even if the two defendants plead different defences an award of damages and costs is recoverable against either of them, however divergent in a moral sense the origin of the libel may have been. A publisher who mistakenly believed in his author's integrity may find himself paying for that author's concealed malice.

Plainly the law could not allow loopholes whereby a penniless author could be hired by a rich publisher to libel a living person and leave the victim with no right of redress except against someone who is not worth powder and shot. At the other extreme, it seems wrong that a publisher could be put out of business by damages and costs that might be attributable to the author's conduct but of which the publisher is innocent in the ordinary meaning of that word. The undisclosed interpolation of additional but libellous matter in the final proofs, of which I have given an example, should surely qualify as the kind of circumstance in which the publisher should be safeguarded from any damages.

A provision which calls upon a publisher to prove that the author wrote without malice is virtually useless, because it is almost impossible to prove a state of mind. I think there should be some reform of the law to clarify what precisely is meant by 'malice' in this context. Better still, perhaps a lead could be taken from the United States Supreme Court and that 'malice' when imputed to a publisher should be defined without an emotional connotation. In a recent article* two members of the New York bar provided a lucid account of the changing meaning of that word in contemporary American libel cases in matters of public interest. A decision of the U.S. Supreme Court concerning the *New York Times* 'defined malice', the authors of the article wrote, 'not in terms of emotion or state of mind (or glands) but in terms of knowing, or reckless, falsity regardless of motive'. In a later case, the article relates, the Supreme Court reversed the verdict of two lower courts on grounds of error by them in definition of malice.

> The *only* definition of 'malice' permissible in such cases the [U.S. Supreme] Court re-emphasised, was the one enunciated in the *Times* case itself – i.e. knowledge of

* Harriet F. Pilpel and Kenneth P. Norwick, 'But Can You Do That? The Two Faces of Malice', *Publisher's Weekly*, 3 August 1970 (R. R. Bowker Company, New York).

falsity or reckless disregard as to truth or falsity. In other words, the presence (or lack) of hostility or ill will on the part of the publisher was wholly irrelevant, except to the extent it might be probative of the publishers knowledge or reckless disregard of the falsity of his publications.

Book publishers almost without exception take a responsible attitude towards libel and do all they can reasonably be expected to do to avoid it both for themselves and their authors. If I could have made the last sentence categorical and not used the words 'almost without exception' it would have been easier to plead for revisions in the law which would reduce the undeserved burden which the publisher so often finds himself carrying. But it cannot be denied that the rare exception arises; a publisher may be tempted to peddle libel for profit not simply for the gain from the immediate publication but for the broader aim of keeping the author on his list. A law that introduced loopholes that allowed irresponsible publication of libel to go unscathed would be bad law, not only because of its withdrawal of protection from those injured but also because truth would tend to become enshrouded in a welter of wild allegations and counter-allegations.

I suggest, however, that there are, perhaps, five measures which would provide a fairer basis for the publisher's accountability in libel cases.

First, that in a consolidated hearing which results in a verdict against the defendants, any damages and costs should be awarded against them separately, so that the awards could reflect any widely different degrees of moral responsibility for the libel if there had been evidence of such disparity.

Second, that 'malice' on the part of a publisher should be subjected to a precise definition (perhaps along the lines now evolving in America) and be easily distinguishable from the personal hostility which, it has to be faced, may sometimes motivate an author.

Third, that in works of artistic creation (novels, plays and poetry) a greater margin of freedom should be permitted than in works that purport to state factual truth; that for an artistic creation there should be a defence for an alleged libel by showing that any divergence from the truth lies within a reasonable exercise of artistic freedom and that this should be a complete defence unless the divergence constitutes a grave libel on the identified person. This principle is already inherent in West German law.*

Fourth, where an 'innocent' (as legally defined) libel has occurred the publisher should be entitled to the procedure of offering amends (in itself expensive) without the absurd condition of proving that the author wrote without malice. It should be sufficient for the publisher to prove that he had published without malice and had exercised reasonable care.

And last, both authors and publishers deserve some protection from ill-founded but determined claims for libel. With the law as it stands the author and publisher will lose some money, even if they are successful in their defence and are awarded costs. As I have said earlier, an assertion of libel is an attack on an author's accuracy or integrity and can be a cause of anxiety and distress; the imputation is less personal against the publisher but the demands it makes upon his time can easily become excessive and the prospects of the book's success may be ruined. Provision should be made whereby an unsuccessful plaintiff could be ordered to pay not only the formal legal costs incurred by the defendant but also a sum of money to compensate him for the related and assessable losses which the measures involved in defending a libel action inflict on the defendant. Until this reform is introduced a defendant, however honourable and innocent his true position may be, must be the loser.

* I am indebted to Rechtsanwalt Peter Sachse of Munich for a private memorandum on this point, from which I quote: 'This comprehensive protection of creative artistic freedom does not imply that artistic expression may be exercised without restraint. For the freedom of art is not an *isolated* maximum value of constitutional appraisal to which all other values are to be subordinated. The right to free artistic activity is limited inherently with respect to the right of the individual which is likewise laid down in the constitution. The limit is exceeded as soon as the image of a person who has been represented identifiably is defaced in a *fundamentally* negative manner by *freely invented* additions, without these being recognizable as satirical exaggeration or the like.'

Five

Eye Witness

Richard Ingrams

When lawyers and politicians discuss libel they tend to think of the conflict as being between the individual citizen on one side and the Press on the other. The Press is assumed to be a newspaper, or a group of newspapers – at any rate, a large, powerful and wealthy concern, well able to fend for itself. The individual, protecting his reputation, is seen very much as a David fighting against this wealthy Goliath. If the law as it stands at present, leans somewhat towards him, then that is all to the good. Behind this attitude lies the assumption that in any event, newspapers are very rich and will not really be badly affected if they have to pay heavy damages.

This is a comparatively modern way of looking at the law. When the laws of libel were first framed, the struggle was exactly reversed. Pamphlets, broadsheets and lampoons were Davids: Goliath was the Government who formed the laws. The laws were enacted to protect the establishment from attack. The attackers were individuals for the most part without money and without power – apart from their pens. Our present laws were framed to prevent these men getting out of hand. They remain almost unchanged.

This point is highly relevant today when we are witnessing the decline of the national press. Newspapers of the old type are dying and in ten years' time or even less there may well be only one or two surviving. In this event we could see a return to the conditions of the eighteenth century – the age of the pamphlet and the lampoon.

The process can already be observed in America. Papers like the *New York Herald Tribune* are dying or dead. In their place literally hundreds of so-called 'underground' papers are springing up – of which only a handful may survive. But they could represent the press of the future.

The reasons for the decline of the national press are no doubt complex. At the root of it, however, lies the fact that the Press has become part of the power structure. To be successful the Press must be divorced from politics and big business. As Donald McLachlan wrote recently: 'The old convention was that a journalist's first duty was to be independent and that his prime role was to be wary of governments and hostile to ministers.' Nowadays the lines are too blurred for the Press to fulfil its historic role. The demands of advertisers, the political and personal involvement of editors and proprietors both militate against unbiased reporting. Correspondents must toe the line in whatever field they specialize in order to be assured of a steady supply of information. In recent years several journalists have been given honours. Proprietors become peers. Distinguished journalists may be honoured with knighthoods or O.B.E.s. Merchant bankers sit on the board. It is all a far cry from John Wilkes.

From time to time Fleet Street journalists or proprietors can be heard making suitable noises of protest against the libel laws. Were it not for these harsh restrictions, they say, the Press could expose the evils of our times. As it is, they must refrain from publishing what they know to be true for fear of legal repercussions. Such heartfelt pleas must be taken, like so many of the emanations from Fleet Street, with a pinch of salt. After all, if a big newspaper really believes in its duty to expose, it can surely run the risk of losing a few thousand pounds in a libel action. No, the Press is restricted by too many other pressures to be seriously affected by the law. The libel laws may serve as a useful excuse for apathy and inaction; they are not the cause. (It is worth adding that the Press's timidity in this field is partly occasioned by the way it chooses to arrange its affairs. Some papers are insured against libel and in order to get their insurance cover they must abide by the decisions of the lawyers who read their pages before publication. The lawyers tend to be on the safe side and as a result cuts are often made which are quite unnecessary.)

To a small magazine like *Private Eye* the laws present a very real threat – and if, as I suggest, we are moving into a period when large dinosaur-like newspapers are becoming extinct and may be replaced by smaller and more vivacious chronicles, then it is high time that pundits stopped thinking of the 'defendants' in libel cases as large and wealthy newspapers and consider the plight of a small and relatively penniless concern like *Private Eye.*

It is a common assumption that we in this country enjoy the freedom of the Press. Compared with other countries our situation may be idyllic but it is not by any means as perfect as some might think. To begin with, a publisher must find a printer and a distributor if he is to survive.

But here we come up against some major stumbling blocks. Under the present laws, a printer and a distributor are liable to prosecution for libel. Nearly one-third of the distribution outlets in the U.K. are controlled by two large companies, W. H. Smith & Sons and John Menzies. (These firms, incidentally, have a monopoly in all railway bookstalls – priceless outlets for any magazine.) It is the view of these firms that, in the case of a small paper, litigants would by-pass the publishers and would sue them instead. As a result they refuse to handle any paper which, in their view, contains defamatory material. Justifiably these large firms do not see themselves as crusaders for free speech and small struggling papers. Nor is there any financial incentive for them to stock minority publications when they can do very nicely out of those they sell already.

The liability of printers and distributors dates presumably from the days of pamphlets and broadsheets when papers changed hands overnight or were edited anonymously. The law took the printer and distributor under its umbrella to make it possible for some identifiable person to be prosecuted. Though it is very rare for a distributor to be sued separately, the possibility is still sufficient to deter these large organizations from running a risk. There have been cases recently where the police have threatened the printers of 'underground' papers with prosecution under the obscenity laws. It is an effective, if underhand way, of harassing a paper, as printers are hard to find. It would be equally possible for a plaintiff in a libel action to threaten distributors, which could result in the boycotting of a paper by the distribution trade, thus killing the paper off. In effect, the law and the near-monopoly position of Smith's and

Menzies represent a formidable obstacle to the dissemination of reading matter. If parliament makes no other reform in this field, it ought to remove the liability of printer and distributor.

The argument of W. H. Smith is based on one assumption which is shared by most of those involved: that people sue in order to get money. If there is no chance of getting money, they will refrain from issuing writs. The common view shared by lawyers and journalists alike is that there are men out there scanning the printed word in the hope that someone will say something about them which will be worth a few thousand pounds tax free. Money is the root of all writs.

This is a cynical view but I find it widespread, particularly among lawyers. Nevertheless, if it were true, *Private Eye* would never be sued and this is far from being the case. Certainly I could instance people who have sued to get money – albeit not very much. But the matter is not quite so simple as the cynics think. It often happens that a statement is printed which is damaging to someone: he may simply wish to see it corrected and apologized for. (It has become rather fashionable in such cases to ask for a sum to be donated to charity, in order to demonstrate one's purity of motives.) Again, a lot of people sue in order to secure public silence on a particular topic. A timely writ will silence a paper and will, in most cases, stop others from taking up the story. There are also people who sue simply in order to gain publicity.

Faced with all these writs and rumours of writs how does a small paper react? Suppose for example that *Private Eye* describes Mr X as a swindler. Mr X, duly outraged, consults his solicitor. The solicitor sends me, the editor, the printer and the distributor a letter demanding an immediate apology, a statement in open court and an appropriate sum by way of damages. Unless these are granted, he says, a writ for libel will ensue.

Two questions arise: (a) can we prove it? (b) can we afford to prove it? This last is the important consideration, for it is the fantastic cost of the law more than its nature that militates against a small paper. Supposing we decide to fight Mr X. We shall need solicitors, a barrister to file our defence, and later on, when we go to court, a Q.C. In addition, there will be the expenses of witnesses. If our key witness lives in America (an old associate of Mr X in his Mafia days) we shall have to pay for him to come to London.

Assuming that the case goes to court it will not do so for at least a year. During this time statements of claim, statements of defence, affidavits, 'further and better particulars', will pass to and fro from the two sets of lawyers and their clients. As the pile of documents mounts, so does the bill. The Q.C. charges at least 500 guineas for his brief and when the case comes to court he will get over £100 for each day the case lasts after the first.

(It is here worth reminding readers whose ideas about court procedure are derived from the telly that lawyers proceed at a snail-like pace. The judge takes lengthy notes in longhand and witnesses must wait for him to keep abreast. The court sits at 10.30 and rises at 4.30 with an hour's break for lunch. When lawyers are paid by the day these points are obviously important.)

The Q.C.'s junior is now paid something over half what the Q.C. gets. Michael Zander, writing in the *Guardian* (7 February 1969) calculated that for a seven-day trial the two barristers between them would cost about £1,800. Solicitors' costs could be double that sum. This is a formidable deterrent to anyone thinking of taking a libel case to court, either as plaintiff or defendant. It should be remembered that the loser in a court case will nine times out of ten have to pay a large proportion of his opponent's costs, as well as his own.

Law is not only expensive – it is unreliable. By this I mean that one cannot sum up the pros and cons and say we will win or lose a particular action. So much will depend on 'how things go in court'. A court action is a very theatrical affair in which performances count as much as lines. Evidence which seems strong on paper can be made to look worse than useless if the witness' bearing and delivery are unsatisfactory. The 'impression' a witness will give in court cannot always be anticipated in advance. Again, there is the chancy business of the judge. Judges, like all of us, have prejudices, and some have more prejudices than others. In the case of *Private Eye*, it is unlikely that a judge would be wholly sympathetic with the aims and methods of the paper. This is only natural, for *Private Eye* and judges are on opposite sides of the fence. The judge in the street, or on the Clapham Omnibus to use the legal jargon, regards *Private Eye* with at least suspicion. He may even regard *The Times* with suspicion. After all, it is the job of a journalist to be wary and critical of authority. And as a judge represents authority as well as any other he is apt to be antipathetic. I am not complaining about this, I am just mentioning it as being an inevitable consequence of the contrasting roles of the judge and the journalist.

As for the law itself, I can only write as a layman, but its faults to me would seem to lie in its vagueness. The law assumes that a man has a reputation, like he has a pair of legs; that this can be damaged and the damage then assessed in terms of money. To take an example, the case of *Randolph Churchill* v. *the People* – one of the few libel actions of which a fully documented record exists in book form:* the *People* described Mr Churchill as a 'hack' – a sublime case of the pot calling the kettle black, or hack. Indeed, the defence rightly pointed out that Churchill had used the same expression referring to the editor of the *Sunday Mirror*. Despite this, Churchill won the action and was awarded £5,000. Whether he was more or less of a hack than anyone else, it is highly unlikely that he suffered any damage by being so described. Did his friends cut him as a result? Was he unable to sleep at night? Did his earnings decline? The idea is ridiculous. And yet a jury awarded him £5,000 to recompense him for the damage to his 'good name'.

It is my contention that the assessment of damage to a man's reputation is far too imprecise a matter to be decided by a court and that therefore it should be necessary for a plaintiff to prove damage. In practice this would mean financial damage – he would have to show that as a result of the libel he had lost his job or that his earnings had fallen, etc. This is the practice in the U.S., a country which has no history of suppression in the newspaper field.

The effect of this change in the law would be to reduce dramatically the number of libel actions. It would no longer be possible cynically to pursue an action in order to get money. But there would remain cases where a plaintiff desired a correction of fact which was potentially damaging if not provably so. For these a Press Council-like body could be set up with

* *What I Said About the Press* (Weidenfeld & Nicolson, 1957).

powers to compel a paper to retract, should it refuse to do so. Such a retraction would carry more weight than many printed today, when papers succumb to threats of legal action simply to save money or to retain their insurance cover.

It is the habit of some lawyers and politicians to view the Press as a horde of irresponsible beasts eager to destroy people's reputations, who are only held at bay by the sanctions of the law. Such a view is totally wrong. It is vital for a newspaper which wants to be taken seriously that it should be believed. The more the idea gets around that you can't believe what you read in the paper, the worse for the paper concerned. Nothing is more damaging for a paper, as I know myself, than the continual printing of apologies, which cast doubt on the credibility of the paper as a whole. Lawyers in their innocence believe that the printing of lies and libels is profitable. It is not. Once the accuracy of a paper is called in question its circulation begins to slide. (It is only fair to add that this consideration explains the reluctance of some papers to print apologies, and the feeling among lawyers that they will only do so if threatened by court proceedings. For such cases, as I suggest above, there should be a quasi-judicial body with powers to order a retraction.)

To return to our imaginary case with Mr X. I have said enough to show that our tendency will be to settle with him. This will involve on our part the printing of a grovelling apology and possibly paying him a small sum. We shall also have to pay his costs which may run into hundreds of pounds. (I have known one firm of lawyers put in a bill for £1,050 costs for a case that was settled within a month of the writ being issued.) There is, as I have suggested, a very strong onus on a paper like *Private Eye* to settle for an apology even though this may not be merited by the facts of the case. There are cases when a plaintiff may demand more than an apology. In a recent action involving *Private Eye* I was told that the plaintiff would drop his writ if we would reveal the source of our information. In other cases I have been asked to sign statements, some of which are quite bizarre. The proprietor of the *Spectator*, for instance, agreed to withdraw his writ on condition that *Private Eye* would not publish any further reports concerning the *Spectator* or its business without the approval in writing of the editor of the *Spectator*. Solicitors representing the *New Statesman* demanded 'a formal written undertaking in terms to be approved by us, on behalf of our clients, to make no further mention in your columns, in any form or context whatsoever, of either of our clients or of any director of our company clients.' Another, from the editor of the *Daily Express*, demanded an undertaking to the effect that we would not publish 'anything in future which is in any way defamatory' of the editor of the *Express*, his staff or Beaverbrook Newspapers Ltd.

It is interesting that all these examples are provided by journalists. For no one knows better than a journalist the kind of pressure that can be put on a paper by a wealthy litigant. Of course, it is open for us to contest these demands in the courts, but at a cost. As the old saying has it, 'Justice is open to all, like the Ritz Hotel.'

Not for one moment do I wish to appear as an innocent in all these cases. Undoubtedly, like any journal, *Private Eye* makes mistakes and on occasion goes too far. For these lapses we should like anyone else make amends. It nevertheless remains the case that in libel the poor are at the mercy of the rich who sometimes use their position to extract money or apologies by menaces. It is equally true that poor people, who are more likely to suffer real damage from the publication of libel than rich men like Randolph Churchill, are prevented from suing by their lack of funds. (It is noticeable how the popular Sunday Press devotes a lot more space to exposing the villainies of small time crooks than those of bigger fish.)

It is commonplace to defend the *status quo* in this country with the excuse that 'it may seem odd but it works'. The law of libel is no exception. Its apologists may admit to flaws in theory but maintain that in practice it works very well. Where these apologists are lawyers I submit that they ought to declare their financial interest in the maintenance of the *status quo*. Looked at from the other side of the fence the law often seems anachronistic, expensive and thereby unjust. Having spent nearly ten years at the receiving end of writs, I hope my views may carry a little weight.

Six

News and Abuse

Cecil H. King

Libel to the ordinary citizen means an occasional paragraph in a newspaper in which some newspaper usually makes an agreed apology in court to someone who claims his reputation has been damaged by something the newspaper printed. Quite rarely a more important case is reported in which large sums are eventually awarded to an aggrieved plaintiff. The casual newspaper reader may wonder why he should be interested in such an inconspicuous corner of the law. But to any publisher what appears to the public is only the very small tip for a very large submerged iceberg.

Roughly speaking, the law is that you may say anything about anyone provided that it is true, and that fair comment on a matter of public interest is allowable provided there is no element of malice. I believe the law in France and the United States is much the same, though the result in operation is far different. The Attorney-General in the last Government when speaking in the House of Commons said he thought the present situation over libel was about right in its balance between the individual's right to protection and the public's right to know. Judges of the highest eminence have expressed the same view. Parliament of recent years has made some small changes: the judges have spoken out against wildly excessive libel damages and the official view is that all is now for the best in the best of all possible worlds.

From the point of view of the editor or publisher the situation is entirely different. He may print or quote any statement made in Parliament or a court of law. But otherwise any statement made about anyone may prove to be libellous and no editor can go to sleep at night without worrying whether or no some libel lies hidden in the columns of his newspaper. Apart from mere accident there are all sorts of statements which a jury may or may not find defamatory: and if they do find a statement defamatory there is no means of knowing whether they will fix the damages at £50 or £5,000.

The reasons for this uncertainty are various. The first and most serious is that any criticism you make must not only be true but you must be able to prove that it is true. I remember once stating in a book that a certain individual was 'pompous'. The publisher's lawyer struck out the word pompous on the ground that if challenged in the courts I should find pomposity very difficult to prove. If a newspaper states that a hospital or a police force is badly run, a libel action will certainly follow. The newspaper may be entirely correct in its judgment and will no doubt be able to produce a number of witnesses to support its case. The matron of the hospital or the chief constable will produce a number of witnesses to show that his or her organization is a model of efficiency and the newspaper will be lucky to escape with £5,000 damages and a further £5,000 in costs.

Of recent years several newspapers have decided to show up some scandal and deliberately court a libel action. One can call to mind the *People*'s exposure of the Maltese brothers and of the bribed footballers; the *Sunday Times*, which showed up the activities of a ring in the antique auction world. But such exposures involve months of work by highly skilled reporters: they often have to be watered down or abandoned for lack of adequate evidence and it is not always clear whether the thousands of pounds incurred by the newspaper in expenses and salaries is recouped in goodwill from the readers and from the public generally. The attitude of most newspapers is that this 'muck-raking' as it used to be called is not worth while and that if the great British public does not want a watch-dog they needn't have one.

But surely the old idea of a newspaper was the correct one – that the Press is the Fourth Estate: that it is the business of the Press to watch what is going on from a very independent point of view and alert the public to any scandal in the public or private sector. A newspaper necessarily is the recipient of a vast amount of information – far more than can be printed – and should be encouraged to use its unique position in the public interest. During my lifetime the operation of the libel laws has become increasingly restrictive in practice. It is becoming more and more difficult to make any adverse criticism of anyone. The activities of the Kray brothers and the Richardson gang were well known in every newspaper office for years before they were successfully prosecuted. One can call to mind a number of financiers whose activities should have been terminated by exposure before they had defrauded numbers of their fellow-citizens. Lawyers sometimes try and argue that there are only a few libel actions in a year and that therefore the problem cannot be a very serious one. But newspapers rarely fight a case unless they feel sure of winning it and even then a glance at the probable bill of costs will often cause the newspaper to settle out of court rather than fight the case and win! For the most part newspapers try desperately hard to avoid libels. In my day at the *Daily Mirror* we had fourteen part-time and whole-time barristers to read the proofs and eliminate any phrases or adjectives that might be held to be libellous.

From the newspaper point of view the problem is two-fold: (1) almost any criticism may be held to be defamatory and (2) the damages are normally so very high. Without going back to the Lewes cases when over £100,000 damages were awarded against the *Daily Telegraph* and the *Daily Mail*, libel damages are normally high. This began with the Youssoupoff case, in which a film company was sued for implying in a film that Princess Youssoupoff was Rasputin's mistress. At the time in Russian court circles this would have reflected no discredit on the Princess even had it been true. However, she was awarded £25,000 and in subsidiary actions against individual cinemas was said to have made the total sum up to something nearer £100,000. The plaintiff was an elderly lady living in Paris and it is difficult to see what damage she really suffered. Then there was the Patino case in which a gentleman living in Paris was libelled by the Italian magazine *Oggi*. Knowing he would get little redress in the French or Italian courts, he sued in the English courts. He was awarded £5,000 damages though the circulation of *Oggi* in England is minuscule and as the paper did not put in an appearance this sum was set by a court official. Then there was the Polish refugees' paper that libelled a Polish Army Officer. The paper is not published in this country and was believed to have a sale here of about 300 copies. Nevertheless the plaintiff was awarded £7,000 damages. Newspaper reports of legal proceedings in this country which are accurate, fair and contemporary are privileged, but legal proceedings in other countries are as a general rule not. It is often unlikely that a libel action would follow the reporting of a case in a foreign court and the damages might be derisory but the possibility has to be considered by any editor. It is far more risky to report what American or French newspapers say about their own criminals – the Mafia for instance. The New York newspapers may quite correctly state that a man is responsible for several murders and is a leading figure in the drug traffic. If an English paper copies the story it can be sued for libel and might have insurmountable difficulty and vast expense in proving the truth of what is quite freely bandied about in the United States. This is the reason why some American stories get so watered down when reported in this country.

The ordinary scale of damages awarded for libel is absurdly high. If you are blind drunk speeding down the road, run over a pedestrian, and totally incapacitate him for life the damages he will receive might well be less than if you impute some lack of integrity to his business behaviour. The imputation may even be true but such evidence as the defence may produce may be disbelieved by the jury. And this brings me to another of the publisher's difficulties. His own witnesses may put up a very poor show in the witness box, but what about the plaintiff's? As so many of these cases are purely gold-digging ones, one may be confronted with any lie however barefaced. Perjury is, in theory, a serious criminal offence but prosecutions for perjury are so rare that perjured evidence is nowadays almost routine.

There are several exceptions, but in cases of slander damage has to be proved and this is normally impossible. In libel cases damage has not got to be proved and the jury can fetch out of the air any figure that strikes their fancy. Judges incline to be hostile to newspapers, particularly popular ones, and juries tend to think that newspapers are rich corporations and can well afford to pay. So the damages of recent years have had no relation to any actual damage done. I would be inclined to say in the course of my forty-five years in Fleet Street that most libels were true and that in most cases the plaintiff suffered no real damage. We have the recurring case of the man who tells a reporter that he is about to marry Miss So-and-so. He fails to mention that he is being divorced by his wife and that he means he will marry this lady when the divorce goes through. Whereupon the wife says the report implies that she was never really married to her husband: that since the report her friends look at her askance as an immoral woman and so on and so forth. One would have thought such friends were not worth retaining and that in any case the old legal maxim would apply – *de minimis non curat lex* – the law does not concern itself with trifles. But not so, sympathetic tears are shed by judge and jury and she collects a nice cheque.

The newspapers have tried to have the law on libel assimilated to that on slander but without effect – or to have the amount of damages subject to appeal – or even to have libel cases tried by a judge without a jury. But they have had no success. The traditional hostility between politicians and the Press is a factor in this situation. Most politicians think they are statesmen sadly underestimated by the media. Most newspapermen regard politicians, with film stars, as the lowest species of human. Trying to be generous they give a few lines to a dreary speech by some vain little M.P. who feels his historic utterance has been slaughtered. So when the newspapers ask for a change in the law their request is received by a profession that is basically hostile. Moreover there are always those with something to conceal who are happy that the present law makes it easy to conceal one's weaknesses – or worse – from the public eye.

If only the law on libel were assimilated to that in Scotland all would be well. There is no reason to suppose the Scots are any less careful of their reputation than those south of the border, but libel is not the nightmare for Scottish as it is for English editors. Sensationally large damages are unknown and newspapers can conduct their business without constantly looking over their shoulders.

That the libel law is regarded as an effective form of censorship is seen by the fact that when a defamatory statement appears in a paper the subject sends in a writ whether or no he intends to fight the case. The newspaper does not know whether the writ will be followed up or not, but if it repeats the alleged libel while the writ is outstanding and the case does come into court, the damages will be even greater than they otherwise would have been. Those who are most inclined to issue writs for libel are not the blameless with an unsullied record to protect, but are usually men with a shady past most anxious that this should not be held up to inspection in a law-court. By issuing a writ he normally silences the newspaper and can then decide on expert advice whether to proceed with the case or to let the preliminary proceedings drag on until the story has been forgotten and the whole matter can be allowed to drop.

But of course the public is not seriously concerned with the woes of editors nor the legal tricks clever crooks get up to to protect themselves. Rather they are concerned with the proper running of the State at all levels and in both the private and public sectors. If, because of the libel laws, a situation is created in which adverse criticism of almost anyone or anything is impossible, then the quality of public institutions is bound to suffer. People seem to think newspapers want to go round blasting harmless people's reputations. But of course this is not so. What does happen, unfortunately, is that any person or institution caught up in a prosecution or a public inquiry gets disproportionate publicity because the occasion is privileged. The hospital management committee publicly pilloried for some mistake may feel aggrieved knowing, as they probably do, of other bodies who have escaped without comment from similar blunders. But the newspapers, debarred from commenting on so much, are bound to go to town when given a chance through the operation of legal privilege.

It is not generally understood how far-reaching the law of libel is. You may not say a subject is being held by the police: you have to say a man is at the police station 'helping the police' when in most cases he is of course doing his best not to help the police. You may not say a company is badly managed or you will be sued, probably successfully, by the managing director or chief executive. So you have to say the figures are disappointing, which is far less effective. You may not say the teachers at a school are not good enough. This may often be true but it is safer to say the classes are too big and the buildings out of date. You may not say a football team is badly trained: you have to say their performance this season has been disappointing. You may not say a professional musician is a bad violinist. You have to say he gave a disappointing performance last night. If a building falls down you may not say it was the architects' fault, however obvious this may have been. You may not hold people up to ridicule and contempt and this serves to protect from comment the monsters who appear from time to time in the news – doctors who, by over-prescribing, provide the black market with their supplies: parents who kill or maim their small children by savage beatings and so on. The mealy-mouthed reports of such events must sometimes give the impression the newspaper is sympathetic to such people. Forthright comment on men in jail is also risky. Whatever crimes a man may have committed he is deemed to have a reputation that can be damaged. If the newspaper fails to prove its case and, as I have said this is often very difficult, the damages even for a man serving a long jail sentence will be far from derisory. In book publishing the law is of course the same; yet, unlike a newspaper publisher, a book publisher has time to check his facts, eliminate defamatory adjectives and so on. On the other hand, with fiction the danger is that someone may claim to recognize himself in some disreputable character in the book and sue. Or the villain in a novel may bear some resemblance to someone the author once knew, or by pure coincidence the story of the villain may coincide with that of a man the author never knew. But the author and publisher are in trouble.

In the literature of the past open reference in unflattering terms was often made to living people and the world's fiction abounds in characters clearly based on actual living persons. If Dickens were to write his novels today he would be crippled with libel actions and injunctions. If he clearly drew his characters only from his imagination they would lack the convincing verisimilitude which is so important a part of his books. The same is true of foreign authors from Dante to Proust. If they wrote in England today they would either have to water down their creative talent or alternatively maintain a discreet silence on the living and only base their characters on persons now dead. Our libel laws have turned the old maxim on its head *de mortuis nil nisi bonum.* It is now not the dead but the living about whom only good may be said.

Seven

A Libel Case as seen by a Successful Plaintiff

Eugene Gros

When one reads about a libel case one instinctively assumes that this sort of thing only happens to people who, for one reason or another, are in the limelight of publicity, either because they are in public life or because they criticize severely people who are in public life. Only too easily is one apt to think that 'this cannot happen to me'. This applied to me as well. Then, one day I found myself in the position that 'it did happen to me', and with a vengeance. Anybody who writes must expect that his published work will be criticized, and of course, this applies to me as much as it applies to anybody else. I am a specialized technical writer and therefore I would not expect that what I publish would attract too much interest outside the technical and scientific journals. Therefore, it was a very unpleasant surprise for me when my attention was drawn to a leading article published in *The Times Literary Supplement* which, under the guise of a review of one of my publications, was a vicious attack on the commercial practices of myself and firm, and on my integrity.

This was the first time in my life I had been attacked in this way and obviously I had no experience whatever on how to cope with this type of situation. One has the feeling of utter frustration when one suddenly realizes that, as an individual with limited resources, one is facing a very powerful opponent with resources which appear limitless compared to one's own. After discussing the matter with several friends experienced in publishing, it became obvious to me that when it comes to the crunch there is no easy and simple solution. One either has to swallow one's pride and ignore the entire affair, or one has to take legal action and then be prepared to fight a very strong and possibly very determined opponent, and risk proceedings which are costly, not only in terms of money, but also in time, personal involvement and 'nerve effort'. Instinctively, I felt that the allegations made against me and my firm in this article were too grave to allow them to be glossed over; I could not just give up and run away because the situation was tricky, in spite of the fact that I had what appeared to me a clear-cut case.

The obvious next step was to take legal advice. This is not as simple as it would appear. There are relatively few solicitors with enough specialized knowledge of libel. Here again, friendly advice from a publishing contact helped to resolve this problem.

I immediately realized that this being a relatively complicated technical case, it was essential to do the necessary homework and give the solicitor the required information in the form of quotations from the article, with my comments, pointing out in each case the true facts or the true interpretation. The solicitor accepted the case and the wheels of justice were put into motion. During this first stage the case appeared relatively uncomplicated with a strong possibility of settlement out of court. The wheels of justice ground very slowly and with the passage of time the case occupied less and less of my mind, although it continuously lurked in the shadows. My position was greatly complicated by the fact that we did not know who was the author of the article and since I never had any previous dealings with the editor of this newspaper, there appeared to be no valid reason for the editor to be biased in any way for or against me.

It is difficult to understand this case without having read some of the facts relating to it. For this purpose I consider it best to quote verbatim the relevant part of the brilliant judgment of Mr Justice Blain:

> This litigation arises out of a leading article – a main feature article – appearing in the centre page of the issue of that journal dated Thursday, May 11, 1967, and headed 'Anatomy of a Publication'. The term 'anatomy', I suppose, means direction and analysis.
>
> As was customary with *The Times Literary Supplement* the writer was anonymous to the reader, and seemingly just

the voice of the paper. In fact this article was written by a Mr. Chomet – a 'contributor', to use a neutral term – who is not a party to this action, possibly because it was not until a very few days before the hearing began that his identity became known to the Plaintiffs and their advisers. He is a man who had worked for the Plaintiffs as a translator for some years prior to 1963, after which his services were no longer required because of the loss of one very large slice of the Plaintiffs' work. (I am not differentiating between the Plaintiff Mr. Gros and the Plaintiff Company.)

The publication, the anatomy of which interested Mr. Chomet and the Defendants, and which the Defendants must have assumed would be of sufficient interest to their particular public to justify its status as a leading article, was a bibliography entitled 'Russian Books on Automation and Computers' compiled by Mr. Gros and published by his co-Plaintiff Company.

The Plaintiffs claim that this article grossly defames them in their credit and reputation (personal credit and reputation in the case of Mr. Gros) and in the way of their profession and occupation and business respectively.

It is not pleaded that every part of the article is of itself defamatory. But it is claimed and conceded that the alleged defamatory part has to be read in the context of the whole, and at this stage, before considering the issues which arise and the history of the matter, I will read the article and the whole article simpliciter as would a regular (or, for that matter an occasional) reader of that periodical. 'Heading: "Anatomy of a Publication". "Mine is a long and a sad tale!", said the Mouse, turning to Alice, and sighing. "It is a long tail, certainly', said Alice, looking down with wonder at the Mouse's tail, "but why do you call it sad?"

'Once upon a time there was a simple dichotomy in the world of science: all the interesting work was published in English, French or German – at least that was the convention – and the remainder could be safely ignored. True, there were distant characters such as Landau, Bogulyubov and so on, but people "in the know" knew about them anyway and there was no real problem. And then, in October, 1957, the first sputniks went up and the situation changed virtually overnight. Publishers and learned societies became interested in almost anything scientific printed in Cyrillic characters and there has since been a flood of translations from "the Russian".

'There are several agencies engaged in the wholesale translation of Russian books and periodicals, all of which are free of copyright restrictions. A farcical situation arose in the fullness of time when the same books began to be translated by two or three different firms and published at more or less the same time. This particular difficulty has now been resolved by the introduction of a Register of Translations by the British Publishers' Association and the Office of Technical Services in the United States. Nevertheless, "duplications" continue to appear from time to time. The situation thus has all the makings of a laboratory farce. There is even a recognisable variant of pidgin English known as "translatorese" ("transjargonisation" being an American term for a particular form of it). To crown it all, there is an unpublicised case of an English language publication which was translated into Russian and then back into English from the translation by an agency which did not at first realise the implications of this for the exponential growth of published scientific information which is worrying everyone just now (it is nearly as bad as the population explosion).

'The explanation is frequently financial. The total capital and running expenditure on science is now so enormous that even a small fractional incursion into these funds, which must, of course, provide for the purchase of scientific publications, yields large sums of money.

'Here is a somewhat exaggerated example. A recent publication entitled Russian Books on Automation and Computers, compiled by a Mr. E. Gros and put out by Scientific Information Consultants Ltd., London, N.W.6, consists of about ninety pages of abstracts of approximately 500 books and sells at EIGHT POUNDS a copy. Analysis of the abstracts revealed them to be competently done and reasonably informative. However, of the

500 entries, about 10 per cent were found to be not of Russian origin at all but translations into Russian of books published in the West. The abstracts are translations of entries from Soviet publishers' catalogues which can be obtained free of charge from specialist booksellers, and no indication is provided of whether any of the Russian books included in this list have been or are being translated into English. A further difficulty is that many of these books cannot be bought even in the original Russian. A spot check on ten titles revealed that none of them was available from the Russian Scientific Bookshop in London, i.e. they were virtually unobtainable except through the National Lending Library (which, incidentally, publishes a list of its own holdings of Russian publications through H.M. Stationery Office).

'Apart from these questions, there is the problem of cost. Our review copy of the "book" was submitted to a well-known firm specialising in this type of composition (in fact, essentially typewriter setting) for an estimate of the possible total cost. The answer was that 500 copies could be produced for a total outlay of approximately £300. Clearly, the rewards of this operation appear to be quite substantial.

'There seems to be a definite need for further research into this field. Since publications of this kind cannot be purchased by individuals (certainly not at £8 a copy) the conclusion must be that one is dealing here with what is known as "library sale", i.e. public funds. There is evidence that many such publications are bought on the strength of the title or subject alone and it would be nice to be reassured by the knowledge that some kind of control (rather than mere automation!) is being exercised.'

The parts of the article expressly alleged to defame the Plaintiffs are the sentence, 'There are several agencies engaged in the wholesale translation of Russian books and periodicals, all of which are free of copyright restrictions', and the second half of the article beginning with the sentence, 'The explanation is frequently financial' and continuing to the end of the article. The remainder, including the title, is relevant background and context.

The defence is firstly that the words complained of were not and could not be defamatory of the Plaintiffs or either of them; and secondly, that those words constituted fair comment on a bibliography of public interest.

The Plaintiffs join issue with the plea of fair comment, and in reply plead that in publishing the words complained of the Defendants were actuated by malice – either Mr. Crook's malice (for which both Defendants would be responsible) or malice of the writer (for which it is said the Second Defendants would be responsible, Mr. Chomet being their agent).

The Defendants say that Mr. Chomet in any event was not in any sense their agent.

Thus the issues, or potential issues, which I have to decide, as a judge insofar as they are matters of law, and as a one-man jury insofar as they are questions of fact, can be enumerated thus:

(1) Were the words complained of defamatory of the Plaintiffs?
(2) Did the words complained of constitute fair comment?
(3) Was the writer, Mr. Chomet, actuated by malice?
(4) Was Mr. Chomet the agent of the Defendant Company so as to make them responsible for his tort (if any)?
(5) Was the Defendant Mr. Crook actuated by malice?
(6) Damages in respect of the business of the Plaintiffs?
(7) Damages in respect of injury to Mr. Gros' personal feelings?

. . . the answers to the first five questions . . . are:

(1) The words complained of are defamatory of both Plaintiffs in the way of their business and occupation and of the Plaintiff Mr. Gros in his personal credit and reputation.
(2) The publication of the words complained of did not constitute fair comment because they were factually untrue and misleading to the ordinary reader.
(3) Mr. Chomet was guilty of malice in writing and publishing the article and in particular the words complained of.

(4) Mr. Chomet wrote and contributed the article, and in particular the words complained of, as agent for the Defendant Company.

(5) The Defendant Mr. Crook was not actuated by malice.

It is a case where the damages must not, of course, be exorbitant, but where they must be substantial. With respect to the libel on the Plaintiffs' business – that is to say, the Plaintiff Mr. Gros and the Plaintiff Company – I award damages of £2,000 each to Mr. Gros and to the Plaintiff Company. With respect to the libel on Mr. Gros as a private citizen for injury to his personal reputation and feelings I award a further sum of £3,000.

There will therefore be judgment for the First Plaintiff against both Defendants for £5,000, and judgment for the Second Plaintiff against both Defendants for £2,000.

My own case was unique; the reviewer singled out a compilation intended for a very restricted range of specialized readers as a vehicle for mounting a vicious attack on firms and individuals concerned with translations and the publication of translations generally, and on me and my firm in particular. This review, which was upgraded into a leading article, implied that we are living 'on public funds' and that what we are doing is so scandalous that it is high time for a searching examination to be made into our activities. My reaction on reading this review was surprise, dismay and shock. I was shocked to see a highly reputable journal with a world-wide circulation publish 'facts' which were not true, and obviously not verified. I was dismayed that I and my firm were singled out for a vicious personal attack by a national newspaper, without any apparent reason. It is very difficult to make a real assessment of the damage such a derogatory article does to the standing of the person or firm libelled. Most readers of newspapers, particularly of 'quality' papers, automatically assume that what is published is true and can be relied on as being true, and that such a newspaper would not single out an individual or a small firm without a very good reason for doing so – 'no smoke without fire!'

There is a world of difference between being offended and hurt by libellous statements which can damage one's reputation, and the ability and willingness to fight a court action to the bitter end. It takes a long time for laymen to realize how serious a matter a libel action can be. In most cases this will be the first time they have become involved in very complicated court proceedings ('such things only happen to other people') and therefore the gulf between their mode of thinking and that of their solicitors and legal advisers can be very great indeed. It takes a long time for the layman to appreciate the vast difference between him knowing that certain facts are true, and proving to the satisfaction of the judge and jury that this is so, even if it is self-evident to people in the particular trade or profession. It is therefore not surprising that initially one tends to consider the solicitor's advice useful, but not taking it seriously enough to prepare the case in sufficient depth. It takes a very long time before a case actually comes to court and therefore the initial excitement is followed by a long lull during which the case recedes into the background and is almost forgotten. Only many months later, as the date fixed for the court proceedings approaches and the preparation of the case is gathering momentum, does the layman concerned begin to realize – very vaguely and dimly – what court proceedings might mean and the tension and mental stresses in one's business and private life begin to mount. It is at this stage that costs begin to escalate rapidly and one has to decide whether to proceed or not.

One great difficulty with British justice is that the law considers everybody equal, not only as regards a man's rights but also as regards his duties and ability to discharge the financial consequences of legal actions. To a national newspaper the loss of a libel case may mean no more than a minor irritation, whilst to the other party it may mean financial ruin and the collapse of his career. Although a last-minute out-of-court settlement is always a possibility, the probability of it happening seems to recede as the trial date approaches. The people around one begin to realize that they are also deeply and inescapably involved, and obviously one wonders often and seriously whether one is justified in taking the risks and suffering the mental anguish involved and whether it would not be wiser to cut one's losses and drop the case altogether.

During all this pre-trial period I was firm in my resolve not to give in, because I felt I had a good case and I assumed that to a large extent my opponents were banking on the fact that I would not be financially strong enough and might quit the arena without fighting. I would like to place on record that during this difficult period my legal advisers acted very fairly, outlining very clearly the risks involved. Of course, in the absence of any gesture of conciliation from the defendant it is the plaintiff who must make the vital decision on whether to proceed or to drop the case.

As the trial date approached mutual disclosure of documents brought to light new facts. Throughout the initial period there were two basic mysteries: the major one – who was the writer of the offending article; a subsidiary one – who was the expert acting for the publishers. Shortly before the trial I discovered the identity of the person who acted as the expert for the publishers. Ironically, this expert was a man who had worked for my firm for a number of years and I myself had spent a great deal of time in imparting to him know-how on sophisticated techniques.

It is during the few weeks directly preceding the trial that the pressure begins to build up in earnest. The hope of an out-of-court settlement fades and the case has to be prepared thoroughly. The demand on your time and resources is growing day by day and it is not only your own time but also that of your staff, your family and your solicitors. As the eleventh hour approaches you realize why in addition to the solicitor and the junior counsel you require the services of a leading counsel. This rams home the message that it is no longer a question of a minor affair with legal costs in the order of a few hundred pounds, but a very serious matter indeed. It is no longer enough to restrict yourself to the facts of the case, but you have to probe very thoroughly and find any detail which may have the slightest bearing on or relevance to the case. In theory mutual disclosure of documents should give you an idea of what you will have to fight and what the tactics should be. In my own case, the disclosure seemed to me rather one-sided.

It is during this period that one starts to work more closely with one's legal advisers and their staff, and one begins to learn and appreciate their point of view. Due to the escalation of costs one also works with a higher degree of concentration, more patience, and the process of learning is correspondingly faster. The importance of communication at this stage between the client and his legal advisers cannot be over-emphasized. The legal team cannot present your case satisfactorily unless they know all the available relevant facts. On the other hand, the client very frequently does not know where the relevant facts end and where trivia begin. It is a pity that during these precious weeks of preparation considerable time has to be spent imparting to the client elementary knowledge about legal matters and court procedure. Perhaps specially prepared documentary films could help in improving the communication between the client and the legal profession. But a subtle rapport, beyond the obvious media of communication, is invaluable.

The trial of my action began on 18 March 1969. The first day was relatively uneventful. I and those close to me (my wife and daughter) had never before been involved in High Court proceedings and we began to get used to the court routine.

At this stage I was naïve enough to believe that the trial would be over in a few days. When consulting with one's solicitor and in particular with counsel, during the period of intensive preparation preceding the trial, when the work is very detailed and, under pressure, has to be efficient, a great deal of work is done in one day. Therefore the layman is apt to extrapolate this type of mental exercise and throughput to the courtroom, assuming that it must result in a relatively short trial. Other naïve assumptions are that the court proceedings are restricted to facts ultimately found to be directly relevant to the case, and that counsel does not make harmful and unjustified allegations which seem to any witness under cross-examination to be wild and cruel although they could become relevant to the case if they do not completely misfire. Both these beliefs may soon be shattered as a trial unfolds.

When the fireworks really start, one suddenly realizes that even the most trivial facts can become important, and once in court one may be obliged to disclose facts about one's private and business life which one would never disclose otherwise. The crunch comes in the witness box, which can be a very painful experience. This is just the time when one most needs legal advice, but is also the time when such advice is not available as one is not allowed to confer with one's legal advisers (or anyone else) once one has begun to give one's evidence.

Since I was one of the key witnesses I expected a hard cross-examination. But before that my spirit sank somewhat on hearing counsel for the defence who gave a sentence by sentence analysis of the text of the article, and his interpretation; according to him, understandably enough, I had no valid case whatever. This did not discourage me too much because I expected my opponents to fight hard and I had no alternative but to fight even harder.

I was in the witness box for two days. The cross-examination began during the afternoon of the first day and soon became a tough battle of wits. There are two incidents which particularly stick in my mind. The first was when counsel for the defence sprang a surprise on me and asked me to translate a synopsis of about 200–250 words from Russian into English in the witness box, and used a stop watch to time me. I believe I translated that synopsis in about 45 seconds, and many people in court were gasping at this achievement. However, whilst I was doing it I did not know whether I should do it as quickly as possible or very slowly, because I expected that counsel for the defence would press the point that if it takes me only so many seconds to translate 200–250 words, then my real hourly charges are fantastic beyond belief and therefore quite indefensible.

Another, much more dramatic, event occurred later in the afternoon, when I was confronted with the fact that a number of allegedly relevant entries, all from a single issue of the source material which should have been in the compilation, were omitted, with the implication that I was not telling the truth when I said that I screened all the relevant source material. I knew I had screened that particular issue but could not explain satisfactorily why these entries were not included in the printed copy. Also, if a mistake was made, regardless of who made it, it is accepted that the boss should take the responsibility, and I felt that this I must do. This episode had a dramatic impact – suddenly my chances of winning the case dropped disastrously. Being in the witness box, isolated from my legal advisers, I was less aware of this and consequently also not as anxious as my wife; in fact even her consultation with solicitor and counsel after the court rose did not bring her much comfort. It was obvious that we were all under great emotional stress. Fortunately, the particular draft copy was found among the huge mass of documents already presented to the court as evidence, which proved that what I had said was true regardless whether an error of judgment or omission was made by not including it in the book.

It is remarkable that finding or not finding an otherwise not very important, even a virtually meaningless, piece of paper (which one could quite easily have thrown away) can suddenly become important enough to make or break one's case: and we knew that some such papers we had thrown away. However, this episode sharpened our awareness and it became clear beyond any shadow of doubt that until the end of the case (the case lasted almost three weeks) we could not afford to relax our vigilance, that we were totally involved, all other duties and functions would have to be dropped and every minute of the day and the night and weekends must be spent in preparing for what might happen the next day. Here 'every minute' means precisely what it says. After the day's session in court ended, we rushed home or to the office. After a quick meal we again got to work to prepare for the following day. Several times this meant for me dictating on tape very late into the night and for my wife to type and amend the text until the early hours in the morning. The same applied to solicitor and counsel. They also have to do a lot of work during the night and it is the quality of this work which plays a decisive role.

One's whole life, business and private, comes to a halt and all one's time and energy must be spent in court and in preparing for the court. One's wits, and mental and physical endurance are taxed to the limit because the stakes are very high, because the costs are mounting up rapidly – at the rate of over fifteen hundred pounds per day (costs of both parties, divided by the number of court days). Due to these costs and the realization that one rarely gets a second chance to present relevant facts, one quickly sees the importance of making full use of every spare moment of the day and night to prepare for whatever the next day may bring.

Before going to court I repeatedly asked why it was necessary to engage a top-flight Q.C. when one had a very good solicitor and a very able junior counsel. After a few days in court the answer becomes self-evident. The battle of wits in the High Court can be very sharp and for the successful handling of a case first-class teamwork is essential; the combined brainpower is not a luxury but can be a vital necessity. We all admired the penetrating intelligence of the judge and during the very protracted proceedings I cannot recall a single occasion when the judge was not fully alert and taking in all that went on in the court. It is essential to feel and respond to this degree of attention and percipience on the part of the judge.

The dramatic episode when I was being cross-examined in the witness box brought home to us the fact that a minor point can completely upset a case, and until the very last minute one does not know if one is winning or not. For anybody who has not lived through it himself it is difficult to imagine the mental anguish and the ups and downs as each sequence of events unfolds and one tries to assess which way one's chances are swinging. It can be very distressing when evidence to prove a given point is readily available but cannot be used because it would disclose confidential information or may involve the private lives of other people. It came as a great surprise to me that facts accepted as valid by the people in the trade and profession must be proved beyond any shadow of doubt in court, from scratch. A case in point is the cost of translation, where 'official' lists of the Institute of Linguists are available in print, and numerous invoices from sub-contractors give precisely the figures which we have to pay for such translation work. This was not good enough as evidence because the fact that I pay a certain price for a translation does not mean that it is the market value. A further bitter disappointment to anyone involved in serious litigation is that when it comes to the crunch and witnesses are needed to testify on one or another point, they frequently refuse to do so (even if they have previously expressed a particular point of view in writing) simply because they do not want to become involved. On the other hand one finds people who are almost complete strangers who are willing to testify on a point which they believe to be the truth, and will go out of their way to be helpful. Even more than in any other sphere of human activity, the human factor plays a very important role in court. Working closely together day in and day out for three weeks in court with a first-class legal team, and watching their presence of mind, is a remarkable and stimulating experience.

Unfortunately, it is only after a certain amount of fireworks in court that the layman involved in litigation realizes fully the importance of preparing the case very meticulously and thoroughly. Somehow I did not take the warnings of my solicitor and counsel to mean that, in very simple terms, you do not get a second chance in court and either you have your evidence ready at the critical moment or you cannot use it. In court, the process of learning takes on a completely new dimension. The enormous court costs and the very high stakes involved in the battle are strong incentives to learn and think fast and to work to the limit of one's endurance and ability. A lunch-break is not for eating lunch, but for trying to dig up new evidence, subpoena a witness or consult with one's lawyers. The evening is not a time to relax, but a time to think very hard of any surprises which may come one's way the next day and trying to anticipate them by giving as much relevant information as one can to one's legal representatives.

My own case was a highly technical one and I was fully aware that, if I was to succeed at all, the technical complexities must be fully explained and denuded of any mystique. I considered it essential that not only the solicitor and counsel should fully understand the details, but the relevant personnel in the solicitor's office should also understand the case reasonably well. I hope I succeeded in this and that I made the job of my legal team a little easier. Anyone who thinks he can win a tough legal battle merely by engaging legal advisers but not giving them sufficient co-operation is under a delusion which may prove very expensive, even disastrous.

The end of the trial came as a great relief, but also as an anticlimax. The hearing had lasted much longer than originally anticipated, and to try to terminate it before the vacation (after which the judge did not expect to be able to sit in the High Court again for many months – in fact he died, sadly, a few months after my case was ended) the judge ordered a Saturday sitting, the first for twenty years in the history of the High Court, but even that was not enough to end the case within the available time. The continuous attendance at the court for three weeks left an indelible impression on my mind; not for a single moment could I relax because a period of quiet was merely a lull before the next storm. When things looked black the persistent question of what would happen if we lost was not exactly encouraging. My view was that when one is on the battlefield one can think only of fighting to win, and not of the possible consequences of defeat. At times during the trial I felt very lonely, despite the very competent and sympathetic handling of the case and the great help from my family and members of my staff. There are certain decisions which one must make alone; all one's legal advisers can do is to explain the possible consequences of one course of action or another. I say the 'possible' consequences because an unforeseen detail may upset the situation completely.

Due, presumably, to the technical complexity of the case, the judge delivered a reserved judgment several weeks later, therefore the end of the period of the actual trial was an anti-climax. It ended the anxious and agonizing moments in court and it also ended the strenuous daily routine of attending court and devoting almost every waking moment to the case, not to mention the several nightmares one had about what might happen the next day. This routine was so enervating that when it was over I did not feel much like celebrating, but much more like taking a few days' rest.

The weeks of waiting for the reserved judgment were agonizing because, although I was reasonably confident, until the very last moment one can never be sure. Also, in cases of this type it is possible to 'win' very marginally but still be landed with crippling costs. Although we tried to stick to our normal routine we could not help thinking about our case and wondering what the outcome would be. Being a pessimist, my wife vacillated between hope and disquiet right up to the day when the judge gave his decision. One may be confident, but never certain. Only as the judge delivers his judgment can one perhaps see which way things are going, and only right at the end of the judgment does one know to what extent one has won or lost. In my case the delivery of the judgment lasted for over two hours, a very agonizing two hours.

The judgment was attended by an eminent professor from

Czechoslovakia who was greatly surprised and impressed by its precision, thoroughness and detail. He considered it quite an experience to see for himself the manner in which judgment is given in British courts. The judges are often criticized because they slow down the proceedings when evidence is given; there is a shorthand writer in the court who scribbles at great speed, while the judge takes down the evidence in longhand – or a condensed version of it. But the result is that the judge has his own thoughts on what is important or not, and when he comes to give his judgment he can condense the real meat of everything that has been said.

I was one of the lucky ones who won his case, and I was also lucky that my opponents did not lodge an appeal. Contrary to what the general public would assume, the fact that the loser does not lodge an appeal does not mean the end of the story. I was awarded costs, but this does not mean that all my costs were paid by the other party, as is generally believed. My opponents did not accept the costing by an independent firm, whom my solicitors had instructed to prepare the bill, which was therefore returned to the court for assessment ('taxation'). Some of the damages awarded to me were used to cover the difference between the real costs and the sum actually paid by the opposite party. Quite simply: the best legal brains one can get charge fees higher than the court will award and to use less than the best is to risk failure. There are of course also other costs. For over a month I and some of my staff were completely engaged in work on this case, and for weeks before that we had to devote a lot of time, energy and thought to the preparation of the case. During all this time normal business was neglected, and during the hearing it was virtually at a standstill. This obviously means a loss of earnings. In addition to these losses, which can be quantified in monetary terms, there are other items on the debit side which cannot be evaluated in this way. The visitor who comes to watch the proceedings for a short period or even for several days, can hardly ever realize the mental anguish and strain felt by those involved, who cannot afford to relax their vigilance and are mentally permanently 'on the go' to the very limit of endurance during the whole of the proceedings. The natural concern felt by all of us at the thought of what might happen if we lost consumed a lot of nervous energy and it took a long time before we returned to normal. Therefore, anyone who thinks that suing for libel is a sure way to strike oil should beware, he may find himself landed with a dry borehole.

The outcome of a case is never a foregone conclusion; surprises are always possible and not always pleasant. I went through with the case simply because I did not like the idea of the Times Newspapers Ltd 'getting away with it' on the strength of their financial power, and because of my belief (possibly quite mistaken) that they were banking on me not proceeding with the action because I would not dare to fight them. Of course, it would have meant disaster if I had lost the case. On balance, when considering the possible consequences of losing the case against what I won, the ultimate net sum though tax free is considerably less than the amount of damages actually awarded; which no doubt seems astronomical to some people. In a way it was a lottery and a very risky one at that.

It would be nice if justice could be less expensive. When the stakes are high, the present arrangement of the team consisting of solicitor – junior counsel – leading counsel – is not a luxury but a vital necessity in a fight with such high stakes. I feel that there is room for changes. Under the present system a plaintiff can have either all – high quality, very expensive justice – or nothing – drop the case altogether. The plaintiff has an alternative, namely, to elect to limit the maximum damages he may recover to £750 so that the case may be tried at a County Court. There, legal costs, with only junior counsel briefed by the parties, would also be effectively limited. Even if there were in any sense a risk of a 'lower quality justice' I am sure that many people would use this alternative if the practical obstacles were overcome (so that a trial might, if necessary, last several days, for instance) and if it were recognized and recommended as suitable for aggrieved parties who are not very wealthy.

What do I think of the British Press? Quite obviously this court case and its aftermath made a deep dent in my belief in fair and accurate reporting of events by the British Press in general, and by certain 'quality' newspapers in particular. In accepting the article which 'reviewed' my book, Mr Crook, the editor, had written that he was 'delighted with the piece'. He referred the article to his lawyer who told him that he must be satisfied of the accuracy of the facts. In his own testimony Mr Crook very fairly admitted that the article was defamatory and that the evaluative comment of the reviewer was unfair. In spite of this he had not checked the facts relating to the evaluative comment, my own and my firm's standing. His inquiries were restricted to asking the writer of the article to confirm that 'about ten per cent (of the entries) were found to be not of Russian origin at all but translations into Russian of books published in the West' and that 'the abstracts are translations of entries from Soviet publishers catalogues', i.e. 'facts' which were not really defamatory and which – as far as they were true – were clearly spelled out in my Preface. I do not know the reason why Mr Crook did not check on the facts which related to those portions of the article which were the most unfair and defamatory. Since *The Times Literary Supplement* has a high reputation and the majority of reviews published in it are serious, intelligent and accepted as such, I can only speculate on the reasons why Mr Crook accepted this article for publication. It is very exceptional, perhaps a chance in a million, that a publication should be sent for review to somebody who may have a grudge against the author. Mr Crook could have hardly guessed that this might have been the case, although when he read the review it might have occurred to him that the text did not seem entirely unbiased. It had obviously not occurred to him that a man might not admit to knowing the person whose book he was reviewing in such an extremely adverse manner – indeed the reviewer himself may not have been aware of his own prejudice. Although we were facing each other in court for three weeks, I know too little about the editor to express an opinion about his motives. His general attitude to the action must obviously have been influenced by overriding decisions of the newspaper proprietors and their legal advisers and there is no doubt that in my particular case his journalistic and even moral judgment could have been affected by unjustified confidence in and reliance on the views of the author of the article, a man with a knowledge in pure science which was quite outside his own literary experience.

What greatly surprised me was the reaction, or to be more precise, the lack of reaction, of the other newspapers. Except for a brief reference in one of the evening papers during the trial to the first Saturday sitting in the High Courts for over twenty years, and a very few lines on the judgment in a few dailies, the case was completely ignored. There is no question that the newspapers were not aware of the case, because a very important point of law was involved which is relevant to any newspaper or publisher, namely: whether the newspaper's responsibility is reduced where the author of libellous matter is not an employee but a freelance writer. So why the apparent conspiracy of silence? It may be argued that the case was not of general public interest or concern. Is this really so? I will examine this question point by point:

1. What *The Times Literary Supplement* writes is of vital importance to many writers whose books are either reviewed or not reviewed in it, and to professional buyers in the book trade who may rely heavily on it. Therefore, writers and others professionally interested in books and literature would no doubt be interested in any news relating to the workings and personalities involved in *The Times Literary Supplement*.

2. High levels of expenditure on research and development are here to stay, and it is obvious that the volume of research and development throughout the world is increasing, and it is becoming more and more expensive. It is also obvious that no country in the world can afford to ignore the research and development proceeding in other countries. The cost, quality and usefulness of this work differs from country to country and obviously depends on the basic policies, organizational skill, available funds, inventiveness and efficiency of the people in the individual countries. Obviously, each country works for its own benefit and does not automatically publish its best and most useful results in English. They also do not supply any guide as to which results are very valuable and which are completely trivial. In our highly competitive world no country can be expected to spend a very large part of its gross national product on research and development and then present other countries with its best results on a plate with a brief memo – this is really very good, the rest you can ignore. Sifting the useful from the trivial is a highly skilful and time-consuming job, of which translation forms only a small part. The problem of processing information published in foreign languages is one

of the neglected and least understood problems of the modern technological age. It is of definite public interest because on a final analysis it is the taxpayer, i.e. the public which pays for a considerable part of the research and development work done in the country. The financial outlay for unnecessarily duplicated research, which could have been avoided by taking sufficient note of published foreign information runs into many millions. This applies as much to the U.S. space programme as it does to other less publicized and less spectacular projects.

Unfortunately, duplication of research effort is much more frequent and costly than people realize, and the money spent on such duplication is in many cases just money down the drain. Usually an article published in a scientific journal is the result of many months or perhaps years of work by a team of researchers, and this is even more true for a book. A chairman of Volkswagen has said, quite rightly, that it does not matter who invented something—as several may do so, almost simultaneously – what matters is who is the first to make a profit out of it. It is surprising that the Press which, quite rightly, devotes so much space to spectacular consequences of costly research, like the Rolls-Royce crash, pays so little attention to the enormous amount of wastage caused by inadequate utilization of results of research published in foreign languages.

3. Successive governments have realized the importance of information published in foreign languages, and have allocated funds for the purchase, collection and, to some extent, translation of such information for the benefit of the British scientific community and industry. The public at large knows relatively little of how these funds are spent and how satisfactorily the department concerned discharges its function. In this court case, one of the people responsible for discharging some of these functions was in the witness box.

4. Since the main theme of this libel case was the charge that I and my firm had encroached on public funds, which is 'a matter of public interest', and therefore of interest to the general Press, I would have expected that the same Press would have been equally interested to report on the fact that the Principal Scientific Officer of the National Lending Library for Science and Technology, who has a considerable influence on the day-to-day running and the spending policy of the National Lending

Library for Science and Technology, i.e. for the administration of public funds, was in the witness box. Surely the personality and the evidence of a man who influences decisions which affect the efficient utilization of foreign information for the benefit of the research and industrial community in the country is a matter of public interest. In spite of that the Press did not publish a single word of his testimony.

Epilogue

When one fights a case of this nature, what makes one fight so hard is not so much to win but not to lose. As the trial progresses, the possibility of losing becomes very frightening because one realizes how much is at stake. Not only can the financial consequences be disastrous – one may be obliged to pay not only one's own legal costs but also those of one's opponents – in my case one of the strongest establishments in the country. On top of that, my professional reputation would have been damaged almost beyond repair.

There is another aspect of libel cases which is rarely aired in public, but which is extremely important, namely, the financial aspects as they affect the parties concerned and the solicitors and counsel. The public should be enabled to realize that when one is awarded costs it means that only a part of the costs are paid by the other party. Therefore, in many cases the 'winning' party has to pay a minor part of the costs which can still be considerable. Another aspect which is rarely reported on, is the financial risk of solicitors and counsel, who are involved in complicated court cases. The outcome of a court case is quite unpredictable. The prospect of a court case being short and successful for the plaintiff may be completely upset during the trial by the emergence of new facts or new evidence which may directly affect his chance of winning and may kill any hope of a short trial. If this happens the solicitor and counsel have to continue with the case regardless of whether their client will be able to pay their fees or not. It is one thing to be able to afford a solicitor or counsel for a relatively short hearing, but it is quite a different matter to be able to do that when the case drags on for many weeks. There is also the possibility of retrial, which although rare, especially in jury cases, does happen, and might have happened even in my own case – tried (exceptionally for a libel case) by a judge alone – had the judge died shortly before instead of several months after giving judgment. In financial terms this would have meant that the costs, which were already very high, would have been much higher, probably doubled. Although this aspect of the risk involved in any such action is rarely discussed, there is no question about it that in a number of cases the solicitors are landed with a part of their fees unpaid.

The toast which one drinks after a case is won is not so much to celebrate victory but to celebrate the end of the most gruelling and agonizing period one can possibly imagine, far beyond one's normal limits of endurance. To some extent it is reminiscent of what one feels after a military engagement, when the joy of winning means more the relief from tension and danger than the joy of defeating the enemy.

The bare fact of Mr X or Mr Y having won or lost and being or not being awarded a certain sum in damages gives no indication of the agonies and uncertainties which the individual parties go through during the hearing, and the great risks involved in the action.

Take your solicitors and legal advisers more seriously at the very beginning. The fact that they advise calmly and undramatically may not be true to your television image of what they should do, but they still mean what they say and much of this is based on court experience with other cases. Also, prepare your case meticulously, neglecting no detail, not only details relevant to the case but also general details which may suddenly become important. Once in court the drama is played 'live'; there is no second chance since a retrial must represent in reality a disaster whatever the ultimate outcome.

And finally – pray for luck . . .

Eight

The Writer and the Writ

Michael Rubinstein

'Books', the court has held, 'are different.'[1] So different are they that, under the Restrictive Trade Practices Act, 1956, the Net Book Agreement 1957 between consenting publishers has been held by the court to be a registrable restrictive agreement regarding resale prices which may nevertheless be legally enforceable between the parties who sign it. But books are also significantly different, as conveyors of libels, from other media of mass-communication – newspapers and, generally, periodicals and television and radio broadcasts. The differences in practice, though not under the provisions of the applicable law itself, are to the grave disadvantage of those principally responsible for the publication of books, the authors and the publishers. This unintended discrimination has been overlooked or it would surely long since have been remedied.

A book will last a lifetime or longer; a newspaper is discarded within a day; a feature on television is a mere flash on the screen, gone in an instant. Should a libel appear in or on any of these powerful media its relative permanence or impermanence might be thought to have a marked and proper bearing on the loss and injury to reputation it could cause, and so on the damages which should be awarded to the aggrieved victim. However, there is a balancing factor in the size of the respective audiences – to be counted in their thousands in the case of most newly published books (even if they are much borrowed from public libraries) but in their millions of newspaper readers and broadcast audiences. Because of this balancing factor the otherwise obvious though substantial differences are, in the application of the law of libel, in practice ignored.

The all-important distinction to which I wish to draw attention arises from the fact that books sell relatively slowly. By the time a libel claim is received in respect of a television or radio programme or a newspaper, the whole deed is done – no expense will have been incurred or income earned in relation to the publication complained of which will not effectively already have been recouped by the completion of the broadcast or the issue of the paper concerned. In contrast the majority of claims in respect of libels in books are made when the publishers commitment, in the payment of an advance to the author, in editing, production and promotion overheads, and printing and binding costs, has been incurred and is at greatest risk – the publisher *must* lose money, several hundreds and possibly thousands of pounds, if a book has to be withdrawn from sale shortly after publication; and such immediate withdrawal is the only prudent response to any libel claim received which is not obviously frivolous. To this anomaly, disproportionately prejudicial to the authors and publishers of books, I will revert later, but it deserves to be emphasized here because in all other material respects the authors and publishers of books incur comparable risks and penalties of defamation with those responsible for the dissemination of libels in other media.

Any given book, like the elephant in the Sufi parable[2] will appear differently to everyone who comes across it. To its doting creator it may be an inspired masterpiece or a flawed pot-boiler; overnight it can turn into a white jumbo of a commodity to its commercial godparent, the publisher, and an unexpected source of wealth for the fortunate victim of a libel in it.

Whatever his book *may* mean to anyone else, no one will share the meaning it has for its author. An author will want every word read and every nuance between the lines understood as widely as possible; for him it does not only represent a capital asset. If the author is fortunate, his publisher will appreciate his intentions and the merits of his writing, according to its kind and the publisher's taste. But the publisher will also regard the book as a commercial commodity; and he must reach decisions, from the logic of his experience or from hunch, on a number of interrelated factors which may be only distantly affected by the nature and quality of the author's ideas.

On the publisher's commercial and production decisions –

notably the size of the first printing orders and the price – as much as on the distinction of the author's work, depends the ultimate profitability of the publication. These decisions will materially affect the size of the readership to be reached, which is of particular interest to most authors; and they may also be crucial to the prospects of doing better than cover costs, which is of similar interest to both author and publisher.

I have tried to indicate some reasons why the author must regard a book differently from the publisher. One consequence is that their reactions are bound to be very different if there should be a libel claim. They do not, as a rule, share the same responsibility; nor can they bear equally the losses resulting from any claim.

Almost any kind of book – fiction or non-fiction – may be potentially libellous. Even historical novels have been used to attack contemporary public figures. An author may libel someone inadvertently or through ignorance of facts or ignorance of the laws of libel; or deliberately, either maliciously (i.e. without a genuine belief in what he has written) perhaps to enhance sales by sensationalism, or from wholly honourable motives – as to expose a public scandal. But the consequences of any claim which follows the publication of a libel may not differ greatly for the author however he came to write it. Although authors as the creators have the primary responsibility for perpetrating libels, publishers as the disseminators normally bear the brunt of the claims, in defending them or in negotiating settlements. It is the publishers, again, who may be obliged ultimately to bear virtually all the losses and there are bound to be some losses even if a claim is successfully resisted.

As I have suggested, an author's interest in his book is not only in the earnings. He is concerned for its success as a channel of communication. The publisher's motives in publishing are more complicated: to a 'general' publisher, pride in producing attractive books in successful, perhaps socially or politically committed lists does not always take second place to commercial considerations. But without overall profitability few publishers can or will remain in business. Considerable capital resources are virtually essential for publishers, but most authors must manage on what they can earn, though not necessarily only on earnings from writing.

It follows that for an author, a publisher must seem rich, and primarily concerned to publish his book so that he may become richer; while, for a publisher, an author may be said to represent talent to be cultivated for its promise. A book may bring the two together, but they are likely to regard the work quite differently, so that it is not the book that binds them but the contract specifying the terms on which the author grants to the publisher his right to publish it. And in the heart of this rose there is a worm – or at least the possibility of a worm: the libel (and copyright) warranty and indemnity clause. As a fanciful judge might say to the man in the dock: 'The jury has found you not guilty, and I warn you not to do it again', so the author, in that clause, says in effect, 'I haven't libelled anyone in this book and I'll pay you every penny you lose if I have.' (And often he may add *sotto voce*, 'You know as well as I do that, unlike you, I haven't a penny to my name anyway.')

Authors accept a libel warranty and indemnity clause in their contracts because they have no alternative. Publishers insist on the clause, even if the contract is drawn up by the author's literary agent. If the author and his publisher were to regard a book identically, the publisher would share the author's concern not to alter any phrase, however unkind or even cruel to someone living, and whether or not that person is obviously identifiable or may be identified in spite of disguise. But why should a publisher's integrity correspond with his author's over this, since it may involve him in the risk – or it might be the certainty – of a libel claim? Unless they share a common ideological aim, a publisher will very seldom care deliberately to endorse the recklessness of an author who considers that he has an inalienable right to defame others and to get away with it.

So publishers insist on a warranty and indemnity clause in all author's contracts, while not necessarily placing complete reliance on it. Some publishers, with a fairly clean libel record, insure against libel risks. Others have certain books read by a lawyer in typescript or in galley or proof and expect their author to accept the lawyer's advice. Some publishers do both. These precautions involve consequences for authors as well as publishers as I shall explain later, in particular when reverting to the all important matter of what the author wants to say.

First, however we should consider the impact of a libel claim – what follows when a book has been published and solicitors' letters are received by the author and the publisher. Such letters threaten legal action for a supposedly damaging libel on an identifiable living person, or an unincorporated body or company, unless an acceptable offer to settle the claim is received within a few days. Usually the remedies demanded include an apology (often an apology in open court), damages and a full indemnity as to costs, and also the immediate withdrawal of the book from sale. Even if there may be good grounds for resisting the claim a publisher is generally advised to suspend distribution at once, to establish his good faith by restricting, even if he cannot altogether prevent, the further publication of the matter complained of, however the claim may go. In the case of some claims which cannot be confidently dismissed as trivial, a publisher may agree to recover unsold copies from booksellers; that puts the unfortunate publisher to immense trouble, perhaps telephoning and sending telegrams, as well as placing announcements in trade papers. And whatever steps are taken it is seldom possible to recover all unsold copies already distributed and all copies sold to public libraries.

The trouble caused to the publisher is bad enough, but stoppage may completely ruin the book's prospects. Unless more than a few pages are the subject of complaint new material may quickly be written to occupy the same space; cancel sheets, as they are called, can then be printed and pasted in to replace the offending ones. This will minimize disruption of normal distribution, and the cost, in effect of keeping the book on the market, may be relatively small.

But often more than a few pages are involved and then, even in the case of a libel claim unlikely to succeed, no quick arrangement can be made to resume distribution with an amended version of the book. Within a week or two of publication the initial impetus of reviews and advertising is greatest; the disruption of sales at this time is likely to ruin the prospects of selling a reasonable number of copies of a book. And the publisher faces not only the loss of his estimated profit on the stock which may never be sold, but also the whole cost of printing and binding those copies which cannot even be remaindered to recoup some part of the loss. So a libel claim itself can cause a serious loss to the publisher, irrespective of its legal merit or prospects.

When a claim is made, the author must of course expect the indemnity clause in his contract to be invoked, entitling the publisher to look to him to cover all losses, including those incurred by the withdrawal of the book. The author's loss of the opportunity to enhance his reputation by the continuing availability of his book may be no less serious for him than the financial burden. The period of days and weeks, possibly dragging on into months, after a libel claim is received, can be humiliating and agonizing for many authors, however it may eventually affect them financially.

Before considering what may happen during that unhappy period, it is worth while referring to the case of a publisher who insures against libel risks, to note how it may differ from the circumstances already described. In the first place, such a publisher normally refers the claim at once to the underwriter's solicitors. They will take responsibility for its defence and if in the course of defending the claim or negotiating a settlement the publisher does not approve, he must nevertheless allow the underwriter's decision to prevail or else forgo the benefit of the policy.

Generally the underwriters will be as concerned as the publisher to mitigate loss and so to collaborate with the author through his solicitors, if it is practicable, to get an amended version of the book on the market as soon as possible and in any event to try to negotiate settlement of the claim. But underwriters can increase strained relations between a publisher and his author. Sometimes an author wishes to resist a libel claim to uphold a principle and, foolhardy though this course may be, his publisher may occasionally wish to back him rather than allow a settlement to be negotiated involving a withdrawal of the matter complained of and a public apology. To seek to justify a libel, that is to prove its truth, is dangerous because of the disproportionate cost of fighting libel actions and the additional risk, in case of a failure of the defence, that the damages will be increased because it will be said that the attempt to justify *itself* exacerbated the initial damage caused by the publication of the libel. Unless, therefore, the terms demanded by a plaintiff to settle his claim seem too high, or the prospects of the defence succeeding seem exceptionally good, an insured publisher must normally deny himself the right to benefit from cover under his policy just when he needs it most if, faced with a conflict between the policy decisions of the underwriters and his author, he decides to side with the latter. Yet failure to support an author in a conflict of this kind can injure the publisher's reputation with his other authors.

An outstanding example of a publisher's loyalty to his author (though not involving an insurance problem) was the Auschwitz Concentration Camp case.[3] In that action, Leon Uris was the author of a highly successful historical novel, *Exodus*, published in this country by William Kimber Ltd. In it there was a passing reference to a doctor named Dering, an ex-prisoner of Auschwitz who had carried out experimental operations on the sex organs of a number of men and women prisoners at the camp. The doctor, who had practised as a general practitioner in England for some years since the war, brought an action claiming that the number of such operations mentioned in the book was so greatly exaggerated that his reputation must be severely damaged, although he could not deny that, as he maintained, under pressure from Nazi doctors who could only have been resisted at the risk of his life, he had carried out a large number of such experiments of which records of over a hundred had been found. Most of the victims had died; some, no doubt, as a direct result of the terrible 'treatment' they were forced to suffer. But over a dozen who had survived were traced and brought to England – from Israel, Greece and America, for instance – to give evidence. The action lasted five weeks and cost the defendants, though they effectively won it, over £20,000. It is true that the jury awarded the doctor a halfpenny damages; but because the defendants had, with a denial of liability paid into court a small sum which exceeded one penny, the costs of the action were by the rules of practice payable by the doctor from the date of payment in. The costs incurred by the defence were increased by the expenses of seeking and of bringing to England many witnesses from abroad, and paying all their expenses while they were here; and the doctor, who had himself incurred very substantial costs, died a few months after the hearing of his claim, without having contributed materially to the costs of the defence which the court ordered him to bear.

The author, Leon Uris, who had steadfastly refused to consider negotiations at any time to settle the action, was fortunate to have the support throughout of his publisher, William Kimber. They must both of them have felt justified in having undertaken the risk and the appalling strain of such proceedings and an inevitably heavy expense whatever the outcome, to see the victims of inhuman experiments at last able to testify against the doctor who had so cruelly mutilated them; this seemed not so much to represent the sour sweetness of revenge as the rightness of truth ultimately proclaimed, and ironically it came about through proceedings brought by the doctor, although at the hearing it seemed more as if he were himself on trial. But no uninsured publisher would willingly sustain losses on the scale involved in that action; and the majority of authors who might want to defend a libel claim on principle simply cannot afford to do so.

An insured publisher, then, is likely in certain circumstances to be tempted to be disloyal to his author. There is, however, a more serious cause of dissatisfaction with libel insurance. When a libel claim is settled by negotiation, as most are, an uninsured publisher may freely decide to what extent, if at all, he will look to the author to indemnify him in respect of the losses he has incurred – the cost of worthless stock and wasted expenditure in promotion as well as production, the loss of anticipated profit, damages and costs paid to the claimant and the legal costs and expenses, usually including counsel's fees, of the publisher himself. The author may have barely been able to pay for separate legal representation (desirable whenever there may be a conflict of interest between author and publisher); and a decision of the publisher to be lenient will take account of such factors as the author's means, the degree of his culpability for the alleged libel and the publisher's wish to retain his goodwill in the hope that losses may be recouped through his publishing a subsequent book by the same author.

If insured, however, a publisher may find himself without a choice in the matter unless he is willing to forgo cover under the policy and to accept liability for the claim as if he had never been insured. The underwriters' natural concern is to avoid or mitigate financial loss to themselves. Even a talented author, with an excellent record and able to protest that the claim could have been successfully defended, can find himself victimized alongside his publisher by a greedy claimant. Yet the underwriters, through their solicitors actually acting in the publisher's name, may 'oblige' the publishers to insist on a full indemnity from the author against all losses; moreover these losses often result from the settlement negotiated between the plaintiff and the underwriters which the author has had no opportunity or power to influence although he may ultimately be expected to foot the bill. In these circumstances a publisher should not expect to deserve a reputation for the fair treatment of his authors.

Let us return to the course of circumstances following receipt of the claimant's solicitors' letters before action, at which point we digressed to consider how the situation may be affected by a publisher's libel insurance. Having taken the troublesome step to mitigate possible damage by limiting the number of copies sold after the receipt of the warning of a claim, there remains still a threat of proceedings. If the claimant wishes to show his determination to pursue a fairly strong claim, he will arrange for the issue of a writ before waiting to consider such terms as may be offered to settle his claim. He may explain that this is not necessarily a hostile or provocative move since he requires a Statement, in terms to be agreed, to be read in open court (for which purpose a writ must be issued) if the claim is to be settled amicably; and only if that form of apology is refused will he pursue the proceedings aggressively by serving a Statement of Claim.

The issue of the writ and its service on defendants, who will arrange for an appearance to be entered on their behalf if they wish to preserve the right to defend the action, are not steps which involve an outlay of substantial legal costs on either side. If a Statement is to be made in open court, however, it will first be settled (i.e. drafted) by counsel for the claimant, who is the plaintiff once a writ has been issued. The draft Statement is then considered and probably amended by the defendants' counsel for his clients' approval and may be bandied backwards and forwards between solicitors several times before its precise terms are agreed. Finally, a copy signed by counsel for each of the parties must be submitted to the judge before whom it will ultimately be read, for his approval. According to the fame of the claimant or the seriousness of the alleged libel, the claimant may insist on the briefing of leading counsel (Queen's Counsel) to read and therefore first to approve the Statement in open court, and in this case the defendants may decide that they too should demonstrate, by similar representation, the profundity of their contrition.

Thus where a Statement in open court is required the costs of both sides, to be borne by the defendants, will be inflated by anything between £100 and £500 or more. The Statement is read, either solemnly or in a perfunctory way according to the style of the plaintiff's counsel or his need to hasten from this ten minute appearance to another court kept waiting to meet his convenience. The judge to whom the Statement is addressed has already read it in chambers. Members of the public may be present, probably by chance, either as drifting onlookers with a legal or a lay interest in the law courts scene or because they are concerned in the case about to commence or one interrupted for the Statement announcing the settlement of the libel action. They will hardly hear or, if they hear, hardly follow and understand the niceties of phraseology which have been so carefully worked out between the parties beforehand. But the Press will have been alerted by the plaintiff's solicitors and reporters, probably from *The Times* and the press agencies at least, will be present. The plaintiff's solicitors hand them copies of the Statement. If the libel is sensational or the case involves anyone famous or notorious – especially in show-biz or politics (in that order) – *The Times* will generally publish the Statement or a fair report based on it and other newspapers also may refer to it.

But there is no guarantee that even a brief report will be published anywhere; and the plaintiff will have no redress if it appears to him in retrospect that the apology read in open court will not have come to the attention of any of those who may have thought the less of him after reading the libel of which he complained. At that point he can of course himself pay to publish the apology, but this would be quite exceptional even in the case of a plaintiff to whom substantial damages had been paid. Some plaintiffs may instruct their solicitors to negotiate for the payment of a larger sum by way of compensation on the basis of the saving of costs if they do *not* insist on a

Statement in open court. An apology to the plaintiff may be made known to the public through a relatively cheap advertisement or he may accept a personal letter of apology from the author of the book; this he can show to anyone he chooses to rectify any damage he believes the publication of the libel may have done to his reputation with friends and acquaintances. Or, as a condition for permitting the book to be put on the market again without amendment, he may insist on the insertion in all copies of a printed slip containing an appropriate correction and apology – again usually far cheaper for the defendants than a Statement in open court.

Meanwhile negotiations proceed as to the sum to be paid as damages. A wealthy plaintiff may require payment to a charity of his choice; a generous one or one reasonably satisfied with the speedy concession of the other remedies he has demanded, may be satisfied with the payment of his legal costs only. To signify the seriousness of a libel, a sum of as little as £250 by way of damages can be described as 'substantial', but usually both parties prefer the actual amount, be it £100 or a sum in four figures, described as 'appropriate' or 'suitable' – it may suit a plaintiff to allow the actual amount of the tax-free bonus to be guessed and the defendants not to have a measure of their humiliation known.

Where invasion of privacy, not at present a cause of action in this country, seems particularly reprehensible and so can be said to 'aggravate' an actionable libel published in a popular national newspaper, the vast circulation and even vaster readership may be regarded as justifying what is in reality a heavy fine by the award to the injured party of substantially more than a few hundred pounds. As already pointed out the promoters of a newspaper or periodical, or a television or radio broadcast – unlike the publisher of a book – will not generally suffer any loss from disruption of distribution after the publication of an alleged libel and the notification of a claim and this distinguishes books from other media, in respect of libels, more effectively than the relative duration of the record or size of the respective audiences. However, there is a pertinent question, usually ignored, as to the impact of defamatory material on readers of newspapers, periodicals or books to whom the person defamed is not known personally – the vast majority of readers except in the case of outstanding public figures.

I suggest that the significant factor is not the relatively long availability of books or the estimated total readership but the circle of people to whom the defamed party is known and who may read or come to hear of the published libel: and that it is the nature or intimacy of the prior relationship of these people with the victim of the libel which is more important than their number. This relationship will affect the impression made by the words complained of, which largely depends on the quality of attention given to them combined with the acknowledged or assumed authority of the source – its 'influence'. Should not the respect due to *The Times* outweigh its relatively small readership compared with the *Daily Mirror* or the *Daily Express*?

A comparison of David Irving and A. J. P. Taylor as historians would be invidious, and possibly resented by both of them; but at present the relative authority or influence of a publication is completely, and I submit artificially, ignored. This is, I suspect, because the quality of attention is such that *most* of what is read goes in at one eye and out of the other – it is without influence! Paradoxically, this negative factor is also invariably overlooked. Sometimes these powerful forces may cancel each other out but sometimes one must reinforce the other.

So much for the flesh and bones of libel settlements arising out of the publication of books. What about the nerves? I have already indicated that an apology in open court may not reach any of the lay readers of the original libel – who knows how many of them will have seen a report of the Statement even if published in *The Times*? Others, who read only such a report, are likely to suspect that there was no smoke without fire, so that the publicity accorded to the withdrawal of the libel may be counter-productive in giving wide currency to a nasty suspicion that the apology was extorted from the defendants in spite of the libel being in fact fully justified.

It may cost a publisher or – if he can pay – an author anything between a few hundred and a few thousand pounds to settle a libel claim. He will know, or soon be advised, that to fight and lose will cost him far far more than to settle out of court; and to take the risk of fighting and then to win will be very expensive since, even if the plaintiff can pay all costs awarded against him, as taxed (i.e. assessed) by the court on the appropriate scale, there will remain a balance of irrecoverable costs for which he cannot be made liable which may amount to several thousands of pounds after an action lasting a few weeks. A successful plaintiff stands to gain damages as well as costs, but if a defendant succeeds he will be out of pocket in any event, and will have been put to immense trouble and anxiety in preparing for and mounting his defence. In consequence, there is an initial advantage to any determined plaintiff because the defendant is tempted to cut his losses, or at least to limit them, by negotiating a settlement in the early stages of proceedings even if he believes the resulting benefits to the plaintiff to be wholly undeserved.

There is a further powerful reason why defendants to most libel claims prefer to settle. As I have already mentioned a defence of justification requires more than an affirmation of the accuracy of the defamatory words complained of: it requires proof, generally through the essential evidence on oath of witnesses willing and able to stand up to cross-examination in court. Even honest men and women prepared to give such evidence may not be convincing under skilful cross-examination; doubt may easily be cast on the reliability of the recollection of diffident or over-confident witnesses, and others through innocence or infirmity may easily become confused. Some witnesses may have died or cannot be found, or the expense of bringing them to court may be exorbitant (as it would have been for most defendants in the Auschwitz doctor's case to which I have referred): others cannot be called without jeopardy to their livelihood. Moreover, there is a real risk that the jury will fail to understand or give due weight to technical evidence and legal subtleties. Legal precedents favour a remarkably permissive attitude towards grossly *un*fair defamatory comment where malice cannot be proved, but the defence must nevertheless establish the material accuracy of all the facts stated or implied on which comment or innuendo is based. Hence the balance is heavily weighted against the possibility of successfully defending a libel action, even when it has been brought to protect or restore a plaintiff's reputation beyond his deserts. Whatever the technical plea, the risk to defendants of ultimate financial disaster is tremendous. As recently as 1970, for instance, in the action brought by Captain Broome against the publishers Cassell and David Irving, the historian, over his book, *The Destruction of Convoy PQ 17*, damages of £40,000 (£15,000 by way of compensation and £25,000 as exemplary or punitive damages) were awarded by the jury to the successful plaintiff and, in addition, the costs to be borne by the defendants must have exceeded £100,000 when the Master of the Rolls' Court dismissed their appeal (but see p. 137).

The pressures I have described, all tending to induce defendants to settle libel actions, place a disproportionately powerful weapon in the hands of any potential plaintiff. Too often use is made of this weapon and claims are brought or at least threatened simply because of their 'nuisance value'; the word 'blackmail' is hardly too strong. For wounded vanity a claimant ought to be satisfied with, at most, a minute sum by way of compensation but he will guess (or be advised by his lawyers) that he might as well hold out for very much more. Authors and publishers are frequently joint victims of claims which do not deserve serious moral consideration but which for commercial reasons they are *obliged* to settle to their considerable loss.

It is against this background that we must return to consider the author actually writing the book which may give rise to so much trouble on publication. In the case of a novel, an author may introduce references to well known people or bodies (such as industrial concerns, shops, charities and so on) to lend verisimilitude to a wholly fictitious story of contemporary life. And experiences of the author himself, or references to events which are known to him at first or second hand, are often only thinly disguised as fiction in novels that are largely autobiographical. An author's description of family relationships and deep-seated enmity between his own projection and a sibling, or parent or former wife, may well render him liable to an immensely troublesome and expensive claim.

Sometimes a publisher will arrange for the typescript of a book to be read for libel by a solicitor before the book is sent to be printed in case there is any especially dangerous passage which it would be prudent to delete. It can be helpful for the solicitor to inform an author, through a written report or at a meeting, how the law of libel may apply to his novel. Authors of first novels, which may contain such autobiographical material, are in special need of guidance in this respect. Often the deletion or complete disguise of the name (and circumstances) of a living person, or of an existing organization of some kind, will remove any risk; but a slight alteration, as for example, from 'Smith' to 'Smythe' is only likely to draw attention to a suspected similarity.

Some of the best authors, drawing on their own experiences have been known inadvertently to leave just one unusual detail unaltered in modelling a character in a novel on a living person, while inventing characteristics, or reactions to fictitious circumstances, which *must* involve defamation. The decision as to what may be deemed defamatory is itself, of course a matter of subjective judgment. A claimant who is advised by his lawyers that something *may* be interpreted as defamatory, whether or not he is seriously damaged or even offended by it, can bring a claim with a substantial nuisance value. Thus the same invented characteristics which may reduce but do not remove the possibility of identification may increase an inherent risk if they can themselves be deemed defamatory; if the lawyers consider that a judge might rule that the words complained of are capable of bearing a defamatory meaning it follows that a jury is likely to hold that those words are defamatory, though it would be as valid to understand them in a complimentary sense or at least neutrally. (In very many apologies made by Statements in open court, as a term of settlement of libel claims, the plaintiff generously acknowledges that the defendant did not intend the words complained of to be understood to mean anything defamatory, even where their publication would have been pointless if only a possible non-defamatory meaning had been intended.)[4]

Far more important considerations apply to non-fiction where the author is concerned to describe historical events, or personal relationships, as fully and accurately as possible rather than to apply a coating of whitewash. Here the distinction between fact and comment may be vital but historical accuracy or psychological fidelity is bound to suffer if either fact or comment is materially modified.

There is of course an infinitely wide scope for the description of an historical event. The range open to any particular author is limited but nevertheless every author except the fanatic will have a variety of viewpoints on personalities and events, and can choose to emphasize one part or aspect of the truth rather than another. Distortion is inevitable: no one can record 'the whole truth and nothing but the truth'. The law of libel, however, increases the likelihood that such distortion, when applied to living people, will present them in a better light than they deserve. At the same time it reduces the freedom of honest writers to question motives or destroy images however much that may be in the public interest.[5] Hence contemporary history is necessarily falsified and psychological understanding rendered imperfect. In these circumstances it is hard to see what benefit is to be derived from 'lessons of history' which are bound to be blurred, or what insight into human motives or relationships can be gleaned from biographies. Historians, lacking reliable sources and secret or 'inside' information from which to distil the truth even about the dead, must rely on hunches, speculation and intuition to reconstruct characters and therefore events. This 'imaginary factor' in supposed knowledge of the past must be an important but incalculable influence on subsequent conduct and, therefore, events.

At the risk of confirming an impression of undue sympathy with the perpetrators of defamation, it would be tempting to examine in some detail the scale of damages and other issues, since appeals against the relatively recent award of £40,000 damages, in the PQ 17 case (*Broome* v. *Cassell & Co. Ltd and Irving*, 1970) were dismissed by a unanimous decision of the Court of Appeal, Lord Denning, the Master of the Rolls, sitting with Lord Justice Salmon and Lord Justice Phillimore.[6] This award, already referred to in another context, has occasioned concern amongst some lawyers with a substantial libel practice and amongst very many publishers. Some of the reasons for this concern will be found in an article by 'Justinian' published in the *Financial Times* on 15 March 1971 and reproduced in Appendix II to this book. The temptation to analyse this case further must be resisted, however, since at the date when this book goes to press an appeal to the House of Lords is pending. There remain a few additional observations relevant to the theme of this essay which may nevertheless be made now.

In summarizing the story of the disaster Lord Denning described a signal directing the convoy, whose escort was commanded by Captain Broome, to 'scatter' as a mistake by the

Admiralty resulting from the fact that 'The First Sea Lord, Admiral of the Fleet Sir Dudley Pound, had convinced himself that the Tirpitz must have put to sea, whereas intelligence reports indicated that she had not'.

The unanimous judgments of the court dismissing the appeals were plainly delivered from outraged conscience. The Admiralty and not, to any degree, Captain Broome, had been responsible for the disaster. But not satisfied to reinforce the jury's verdict in the cause of historical accuracy the occasion was taken to make legal history. The court courageously – and unanimously – considered that the unanimous House of Lords decision in *Rookes* v. *Barnard*[7] which put exemplary damages 'in a strait-jacket' and 'knocked down the common law as it had stood for centuries' was reached *per incuriam* (i.e. through oversight, or lack of care). Their Lordships did not mince their words in expressing extremely unflattering opinions of the defendants. But then neither were the terms flattering in which the court referred, in passage after passage, to the decision of Lord Devlin, endorsed by all *his* colleagues in *Rookes* v. *Barnard*. One was inescapably reminded of the indictment of the Royal Navy on the blurb of Mr Irving's book for 'blunders, mis-calculations and misunderstandings', for which Lord Denning had expressly condemned Cassell's.

But, with the cheering thought that 'frailty thy name is man' as well as woman, one is left with a resounding reinforcement of the law of libel as it stands today (in relation to exemplary damages with the pre-1964 position even restored), and of the influential Establishment view that there is no present call for its reform. As *The Times* reported, Lord Denning with characteristic modesty said that he was

> conscious that he might be at fault. Some would say that it was their Lordships' duty to follow the House of Lords. If that were so the case must be considered on the footing that the Court was bound by *Rookes* v. *Barnard*. Counsel for both defendants had submitted that there was no case for exemplary damages under the category of calculation of profit. His Lordship would agree that on a narrow interpretation of Lord Devlin's words there was not such evidence. But that category should be construed broadly to

include all cases where the defendant knew his words were or might be libellous and yet took his chance because of the profit he hoped to make from the book as a whole.

Lord Denning is widely respected for his invariable humanistic as distinct from legalistic approach to every aspect of every appeal made to his court which lends itself to this alternative. Even where he is in a minority on this account so that his judgments do not prevail, or where his decisions are overruled in the House of Lords, it is an inestimable benefit to the standing of the judicature in this country and the respect that it has rightly earned throughout the world, to have so brilliant and lively a mind refusing the confinement of tradition where it seems to him to contradict some element of natural justice. Nevertheless, in practice, there is a concomitant disadvantage in such unpredictability. Who could have calculated that a *narrow* interpretation of Lord Devlin's words concerning exemplary damages under the category of calculation of profit would not apply? Publishers are hard-pressed enough as it is to feel confident of the reliability of any calculation of profit in ordinary publishing decisions: what reliance can they now place on any calculations of legal interpretation, when this may turn a marginal and uncertain profit of a few thousand pounds into a swingeing loss of over one hundred thousand pounds? (In case the House of Lords, given the opportunity, were after all to hold that *Rookes* v. *Barnard* did apply, Lord Denning expressed it as his view that the summing-up to the jury was faulty on a strict construction but preferred, in relation to that aspect of the matter also, to take a broad view . . .) Captain Broome's case has floodlighted the publisher's dilemma. And what of the author who had had the temerity to write about historical events which occurred when, as Lord Denning emphasized, he was only a small boy? From several years of intensive research and writing he could at best have hoped to receive only a few thousand pounds 'profit' even if his book were sensationally successful; and then he was facing possible bankruptcy from the imposition of legal penalties and costs. Cold comfort for him to be pilloried in the eminent company of Admiral of the Fleet Sir Dudley Pound and Lord Devlin.

One important point at issue has as such, nothing to do with

Captain Broome or Cassell's and David Irving as the parties to a libel action subjected, as so few are, to the full test of trial by jury. But it has everything to do with the principle of trial by jury for libel claims as the basis for assessing appropriate awards of damages. Awards of damages by judges in personal injury actions are often compared with those determined, almost always by juries, in libel actions. To the lay reader of inevitably brief reports in newspapers, it may seem astonishing that alleged damage to reputations or hurt feelings can and so often do rate a higher level of compensation than injuries which cause permanent disability.

No less relevant to the issue is a comparison of awards by juries of damages for libel with fines imposed by judges on those convicted, otherwise than by a court of summary jurisdiction, of serious motoring offences or of fraud.* For dangerous driving resulting in death or injury a fine of £500 or more, even without a prison sentence, would be exceptional. And in these criminal cases, while the verdict is left to the jury, the judge alone and not the jury is trusted to pronounce the sentence (a fine and/or imprisonment) and, in the case of a fine, to decide on the amount – which is often restricted by statute. But when a man asks the court to place a monetary value on the harm done to his good name or to his feelings by something published in a book (or elsewhere) the matter is left to a jury. Since the compensation awarded to the successful litigant is in effect a fine 'punishing' the unsuccessful defendant, comparison with the fines imposed on those convicted of crimes (for whom the liability for costs is at the same time disproportionately small) is pertinent. In this area, self-evidently, 'there ain't no justice'. There is good reason for the view of many that libel damages should be determined by judges. In the PQ 17 case, however, Lord Justice Salmon indicated that he regarded it as right for a jury to award libel damages, and that if sometimes a jury awarded more than a judge would have done there was no need for the restraints of *Rookes* v. *Barnard* since the Court of Appeal had ample power to deal with a totally unreasonable award of a jury: but the risk of adding a burden of twenty

* Though Lord Justice Salmon has quoted with approval a dictum of Lord Atkin to the effect that there is no analogy between exemplary damages and a sentence of a fine on conviction for a crime.

thousand pounds or so in costs to the jury's award of damages considered excessive and the costs of the trial itself *must* deter most aggrieved parties from appealing at all.*

Members of a jury have only the guidance of a judge's summing-up, which, while often illuminating the judge's personal bias by the use of dramatic inflections not apparent from the transcript possibly later to be considered by a Court of Appeal, is necessarily too vague on the issue of punishment to help them in deciding on the amount of damages to award in a libel action; they cannot call on the experience of libel lawyers who know what is involved financially, in practice, in contested libel actions and in negotiations for settlement out of Court, and indeed even the trial judge may lack such experience. While the right to insist on damages, which strengthens his hand in negotiations, may be waived in negotiations for a settlement out of court by a generous or wealthy claimant, or powerful defendants may be able to force a poor claimant to accept a nominal or a modest sum (up to £100, for instance), compensation of between £250 and £1,000 is normally accepted as reasonable. Even a libel imputing criminal, perverted or grossly corrupt conduct or motives to someone in a position of public responsibility is unlikely to be settled for a figure in excess of £2,500. Against this background of compensation generally accepted as adequate when libel actions are settled by negotiation, of which the layman is almost certainly ignorant, the well-publicized awards by juries of five-figure damages are particularly prejudicial to any defendant at the trial of a libel action.

In theory it would seem reasonable that an honest and careful author should be free to write critically about a living person or an existing organization. Would such freedom open the way for an unscrupulous author carelessly or recklessly to harm his chosen victim, or to attack any cause he identified with that victim? There are certainly a few instances of libel claims, some settled and some ultimately going to trial, where the claimant deserves substantial compensation for unwarranted and reckless or malicious denigration, even where actual loss cannot be

* See the strength of other similar views described by Mr H. Montgomery Hyde on p. 29.

quantified and proved as 'special damages': as we have seen, the Court of Appeal considered Captain Broome's to be such a claim. It may well be, however, that the vast majority of libel claimants would be fairly recompensed and should be satisfied with a modest sum paid reasonably soon after the offending publication, together with the other moderate remedies referred to in a leading article published in *The Times Literary Supplement* on 11 October 1963 under the title, 'Let there be libel?' This suggested that unless special damage were proved an award of damages in respect of libel might be limited to £250, or even as little as £100,* while newspapers and periodicals with large circulations could pay rather more for careless or deliberate defamation.† It was pointed out in the article that, to everyone's advantage, '*a much reduced scale of compensation would perhaps deflate the assumed gravity of libel*'. This seems to me a crucial principle for any approach to the reform of the law relating to defamation. Apart from compensation, there could be a public apology and withdrawal or correction without the disproportionate cost of a Statement in open court – barely 'public' anyway unless reproduced in a newspaper – by publication in not more than two or three column inches in the personal columns of three national or local newspapers. The article concluded:

> With the resulting limitations on legal costs (even in cases which might still be brought or fought in the High Court) Legal Aid not at present available in respect of defamation proceedings, could be extended so that poverty would no longer deny legal redress to anyone injured by a libel, or to an impoverished author obliged to defend a claim. Any defamatory passage should if possible be deleted or amended in all subsequent printings of the book, or else it should not be republished, except by agreement with the claimant, when the libellous edition is sold out.

* In the PQ 17 case Lord Justice Salmon expressed the view hardly open to dispute, that any ceiling, high or low, being artificial was liable in some cases to be too high or too low.

† This would narrow the remedies for libel as for slander, in contrast to the distinguished academic legal opinions cited by Mr H. Montgomery Hyde on pp. 27–8.

A natural concern to remove certain anomalies which make publishers and authors liable to pay damages in excess of a claimant's deserts, and to incur disproportionate costs in resisting or settling a claim, must not be allowed to distract from the real issue of the law of libel in relation to literary works as distinct from the products of journalism. Probably the majority of libel claims in respect of books result from ignorance or carelessness rather than from deliberate or reckless malice on the part of authors. Nevertheless, generally, authors have a direct 'moral' responsibility for the publication of libels not shared by their publishers although the latter must accept a share – often a heavy share – of the legal responsibility. In appealing against the award of £25,000 exemplary damages in the PQ 17 case Cassell's claimed that should that appeal fail the award should be apportioned, because Mr Irving was more deserving of punishment than they were. Lord Denning, however, did not think there was much to choose between them ('the pot calling the kettle black') and in any case confirmed that 'the law was settled that as against joint tortfeasors the jury must assess one sum of damages against all defendants, even though one was more guilty than the other. That might seem unfair to the least guilty, but it was so well settled that only the legislature could alter it.' The Publishers' Association should perhaps be asked to provide a 'Short Guide for the Avoidance of Indefensible Libels' which publishers should require authors to read before (and after) signing a publishing contract with its libel warranty and indemnity clause.

The psychology of libel-prone authors might usefully be the subject of expert study. No less interesting, however, would be an examination of the psychology of libel claimants. Sometimes an unwarranted libel really can damage an honest business or professional career, though claims in this category more often arise out of publication in a newspaper than a book. But the majority of claimants are those whose precious 'reputations' *may* have been damaged, or who claim to have suffered from hurt feelings. They have been held up to hatred, ridicule and contempt – or lowered 'in the estimation of right-thinking members of society generally'[8] – the very words are redolent of an outmoded Victorian hyper-sensitivity relying on a concept wholly at variance with contemporary understanding of social psychology, to say nothing of the teachings of the Bible. Are those who most easily take offence also in some ways more vulnerable? Who amongst us is so perfect as to be above all criticism? And (to be unreasonably puritanical) what imputation of unworthy motives, if not acts, would really be unjust were all our thoughts as well as actions known? If adultery (and any other sin, or any mean or evil conduct, or foolishness) may be committed in the mind, can there be such a thing, in reality, as defamation of character?

After this string of rhetorical questions, let me pose a practical one. According to existing procedures, on an application for an injunction provision may be made to compensate the party to be restrained by the injunction if it were granted but that party were ultimately to win at the trial. Why then should not both publishers and authors be given a new and specific statutory right – a right to counterclaim for damages, including the losses caused by the disruption of publication on receipt of a claim, and damage to their reputations, in any libel action other than one in which a claim for special damages only is pleaded? Such a counterclaim might be allowed to succeed whatever the result of the libel claim itself. That should help to restore balance to the administration of justice, if our society is not yet mature enough to treat insults with the same indulgence as flattery.

Flattery, such as the adulation accorded to a pop star or a footballer, is regarded as fine, even if it nauseates some who know his personal life to be less than admirable. Unmerited praise makes many people uncomfortable: but do we react to undeserved criticism more violently than to criticism we know to be valid? As we all have human weaknesses, everyone should perhaps have a right to elect that his failings shall remain secret unless he choose otherwise. It is undoubtedly harder for some people to bear a just accusation than an unjust one,* but the law gives protection at present, in the form of penal remedies, almost equally in either case, so that, no doubt

* 'Useful men, carrying on useless work, do not become angry if they are called useless. But the useless who imagine that they are operating in a significant manner become greatly infuriated if this word is used about them.' From 'The Journeys of Kazwini' in *Thinkers of the East* by Idries Shah, 1971.

unintentionally, *anyone* may be compensated who is referred to in terms which might offend him. It is as if we don't want people to be upset by *anything* published; and as if the ultimate horror for anyone is the fear of being 'lowered in the estimation of right-thinking people'. Who are these 'right-thinking people' – are they perhaps the mirror-image of the fearful, guilt-ridden side of each of us, too weak to face the truth about ourselves?

The crisis of our time is a crisis of communication – communication not merely between generations or ideologies, but between the protagonists in society, and often at one time or another in each one of us, for mutually exclusive and contradictory attitudes of mind. These may be categorized as support, on the one hand, for what is traditionally taken for granted as 'right' (law and order, success, morality) and, on the other, for what is idealized as freedom, for 'doing your thing' (shades of Aleister Crowley!). A reliance on self-knowledge is to be contrasted with 'the estimation of right-thinking people'; what 'right-thinking people' take for granted, from this point of view, involves hypocrisy on a vast scale. And those who today campaign for freedom in the name of 'love' see themselves in a world (a world apart?) where 'it's self-*deception* that makes the world go round'. Our law of libel ensures that self-respect depends on public respect. In a maturing society it is perhaps time to trust conscience a little more, and to cease to invoke hush-money in reverse – a threat of writ and damages – to keep Britain safe for complacency and humbug.

References

1 *In re* Net Book Agreement 1957 (1963) L.R. 3 R.P. 246; [1962] 1 W.L.R. 1347; [1962] 3 All E.R. 751.
2 See *The Dermis Probe* by Idries Shah (Cape 1970).
3 *Dering* v. *Uris and William Kimber Ltd* [1964] 2 All E.R. 60.
4 See Mr Montgomery Hyde's comment on *Capital and Counties Bank* v. *Henty* (1882), p. 8.
5 See Mr H. Montgomery Hyde on *R.* v. *Topham* (1971), p. 23.
6 [1971] 2 All E.R., p. 187, C.A.
7 [1964] 1 All E.R., p. 767, H.L.
8 Per Lord Atkin in *Sim* v. *Stretch* (1936) 52 T.L.R. at p. 671.

Nine

Defamation as Contempt of Parliament

Louis A. Abraham, C.B., C.B.E.

The House of Commons has from a very early date treated speaking words or publishing writings defamatory of the House or of a member or members as a breach of its privileges.* In 1559 we find the House committing one William Thrower to the custody of the Serjeant at Arms for a contempt in words against the dignity of the House, and in 1580 Arthur Hall, a member, was imprisoned, fined and expelled by the House for 'publishing . . . a libel . . . containing matter of infamy of sundry good particular members of the House and of the whole state of the House in general, and also of the power and authority of the House; affirming that he knew of his own knowledge that the House had de facto judged and proceeded untruly.' On 28 February 1702 the House resolved 'that to print, or publish any books or libels, reflecting upon the proceedings of the House of Commons, or any member thereof, for or relating to his service therein, is a high violation of the rights and privileges of the House of Commons.'

In the seventeenth century the House was highly sensitive about its dignity and that of its members. In 1680 Joseph Padgett, a parson, who in a coffee house appended the comment 'a damnable lie' to one entry in a copy of the votes of the House, printed by order of the House, and 'voted like rogues' to another, was ordered to be sent for in custody. In 1690

* The term 'breach of privilege', properly applicable only to one species of contempt of Parliament, viz. breach of the privilege of members from arrest in civil suits, has long been applied to the whole genus. The most probable explanation for this inaccurate and indiscriminate use of the term is that breach of the privilege of arrest, as it was the earliest, so it long remained the most frequent offence with which the House of Commons was called upon to deal.

William Briggs for saying of a member 'God damn Sir Jonathan Jennings; he did not care a fart for him; he thought himself as good a man as he; nor did he care for the parliament nor committee', was committed to the custody of the Serjeant at Arms, and the like punishment was inflicted in 1696 on one Markham who boasted that he had been before a committee of the House, but 'they were all a company of hot headed fools and could do nothing with him; and that he came off with flying colours'.

In recent years, complaints of breach of privilege by defamation of the House or members of the House have been not only more numerous than complaints of any other species of this offence, but exceed in number all other complaints of breach of privilege. Between 1900 and 1970 of the fifty-seven complaints of breach of privilege which were either disposed of summarily by the House or referred to the Committee of Privileges, thirty-seven were complaints of defamatory speeches or writings as compared with twenty complaints of other species of breach of privilege.

Since 1940 complaints of breach of privilege have almost invariably been referred to the Committee of Privileges and the conclusions reached by that Committee and embodied in their reports are often spoken of as if they were on a par with decisions of the House itself. It is therefore necessary to emphasize that a report of the Committee of Privileges, though entitled to respect, remains an expression of their opinion only unless and until it is adopted by the House. It is true that when the Committee of Privileges has recommended the House not to take any further action with regard to a complaint, the House has invariably taken their advice. But a report from the Committee stating that they do not consider that the act complained of is a breach of privilege cannot be regarded as having been tacitly accepted by the House because the report has been presented to the House and ordered to lie upon the table and to be printed, as some have asserted. Owing to the manner in which reports of committees are presented to the House, the House has no opportunity of refusing to receive a report of whose contents it is necessarily ignorant, and the orders that the report do lie upon the table and be printed are 'orders of course'. Indeed, in cases where the Committee of Privileges has made such a report, the Leader of the House has, to the writer's knowledge, more than once been advised by the authorities of the House not to move the House to agree to the report, but to leave the House free to reconsider the question should a similar case arise.

Cases of breach of privilege by reflections on proceedings of the House of Commons, frequent in the seventeenth and eighteenth centuries, are now comparatively rare. By 1861 Erskine May could say:[1]

> Rarely has either House thought fit, of late years, to restrain by punishment even the severest censures upon its own debates and proceedings. When gross libels have been published upon the House [of Commons] itself or any of its members, the House has occasionally thought it necessary to vindicate its own honour by the commitment of the offenders to custody. But it has rightly distinguished between libels upon character and motives and comments, however severe, upon political conduct.

The last instance of a libel on a proceeding of the House occurred twenty years ago. On 23 November 1950 the attention of the House was drawn to an article in the *Manchester Guardian* containing a report of a speech delivered by Mr Warnock, the Attorney-General of Northern Ireland. According to this, Mr Warnock had described the decision of the House that the election of Mr MacManaway, an ordained priest of the Church of Ireland, for Belfast West, was void and that a new writ should be issued, because he had been at the time of his election, and still was, incapable of sitting and voting in the House of Commons by reason of the provisions of the House of Commons (Clergy Disqualification) Act, 1801 as 'a dirty political trick', adding that Mr MacManaway had been put out, not because he was a clergymen, but because the Socialist Party saw a way of using an old Act of Parliament to increase their slender majority from six to eight. At the Speaker's request, the matter was deferred till the next sitting in order to give him more time to consider the question. When consideration of the matter was resumed next day, the Speaker informed the House that he had received a telegram from Mr Warnock stating that he had caused a statement to be inserted in the evening papers on 23

November to the effect that his allegations were unjust and ought not to have been made, and that he wished to withdraw them, and assuring the Speaker that he had not intended to reflect on the House or on the propriety of its action, and tendering 'a very humble and a very sincere apology' to the Speaker, and through him, to the House, for the words he had used. The House thereupon resolved that Mr Warnock had been guilty of a breach of privilege, but that the House, having regard to the full and ample apology he had offered, would not proceed further in the matter.

It is sometimes said that reflections on the character of the House, as well as reflections on its proceedings, are breaches of privilege. What is meant by a reflection on the character of the House is not clear. The character of the House can be nothing but the character of the members who compose it. Possibly the expression is intended to cover allegations such as the statement that 'the acceptance of bribes by members is in accordance with the sacred traditions of the House of Commons' which was held in 1930 to be a gross libel on the House.

Reflections on members of the House generally are regarded as reflections on the House itself. In 1956 a complaint was referred to the Committee of Privileges concerning an article in a Sunday newspaper headed 'Privilege', alleging that 'politicians' were getting 'prodigious supplementary allowances' of petrol under the petrol rationing scheme, and asking what M.P.s were doing about 'this monstrous injustice', adding that 'if politicians are more interested in privileges for themselves than in fair shares for all, let it be made plain to them that the public do not propose to tolerate it.' The Committee reported that 'politicians' would ordinarily be understood to mean, primarily though not exclusively, members of Parliament, that in their view the article clearly meant, and was intended to mean, that members of Parliament were getting an unfair allocation of petrol, and was intended to hold them up to public obloquy on account of their alleged failure to protest against an unfair discrimination of which they were beneficiaries. By alleging that members of the House had been guilty of contemptible conduct in failing, owing to self-interest, to protest against an unfair discrimination in their favour, the editor, the Committee said, had reflected upon all members of the House and so upon the House, and had therefore committed a serious contempt.

But although reflections upon unidentifiable members may be so phrased as to amount to a reflection upon the House itself, the statement in May's *Parliamentary Practice* (17th ed., p. 118) that 'reflections upon members, the particular individuals not being named or otherwise indicated, are equivalent to reflections on the House', which appeared for the first time in the fourteenth edition of that treatise, goes too far. The editor cannot have meant to say that a reflection upon members, however few in number, would be equivalent to a reflection upon the House, merely because the members against whose conduct the imputation was directed were unidentifiable.

The principle upon which reflections upon the character or proceedings of the House are treated as breaches of privilege is that by diminishing the respect due to the House they lessen its authority and so obstruct or impede it in the performance of its functions. Reflections upon the character or conduct of members, on the other hand, are regarded as offences of the same species as assaults upon, or insulting behaviour to, members on account of their conduct in Parliament. Molestation of members on account of their conduct in Parliament is treated as a breach of privilege because it tends or may tend to impair their independence in the future performance of their duties. Reflections upon the character or conduct of members, though they do not operate by physical force, yet by bringing them into public odium or contempt, have much the same effect as physical molestation. As Mr Justice Frankfurter observed in *Tenney* v. *Brandhove*, 'one must not expect uncommon courage even in legislators'.[2]

However extravagantly the House may have used its power of committing for breaches of its privileges or other contempts of its authority or dignity in the seventeenth and eighteenth centuries, it does not seem ever to have claimed that *any* aspersion upon the conduct of one of its members, irrespective of whether it related to his parliamentary conduct or not, would constitute a breach of privilege. Not until 1863 did Erskine May think it advisable to lay it down that 'to constitute a breach of privilege [libels upon members] must concern the character or conduct of members in that capacity'.[3] The expression 'character or conduct of a member in his capacity as a member' is not self-explanatory, and the examples May gave in later editions of his treatise of aspersions upon the conduct of members which were not fit subjects for complaint to the House of Commons, viz. aspersions upon their conduct as magistrates, officers in the army or navy, counsel or employers of labour, or in private life, or otherwise than in relation to Parliament, were obviously not exhaustive. There are many acts which the man in the street would regard as done by members in their capacity as members, e.g. taking up their constituents' grievances with the appropriate minister or with local authorities, imputations in respect of which would not be treated as breaches of privilege. In 1887 Mr Speaker Peel refused to give precedence over the orders of the day to a complaint by Sir Wilfrid Lawson concerning an article in *The Times* because, he said, the rule was 'that in order to raise a case of privilege the imputation must refer to the action of members in the discharge of their duties in the actual transaction of the business of the House'.*

Although the reasons assigned by Speakers for refusing to give priority to a complaint of breach of privilege over the business of the day are dicta only – only the House can decide whether a particular act is or is not a breach of privilege – Mr Peel's statement was accepted as correctly stating the rule, and in the next edition of May's treatise the words 'and the libel must be based on matters arising in the actual transaction of the business of the House' were added to the statement that 'in order to constitute a breach of privilege libels upon members must concern the character or conduct of members in that capacity'.

In 1947, however, an inroad was made on the rule. On 16 April a complaint concerning an article in a weekly newspaper

* The words complained of were not, as is often said, the allegation that certain members 'drew their living and their notoriety from the steady perpetration of crimes to which civilisation decreed the gallows', or that 'their political existence depended on an organised system of midnight murder', but that 'history would record with amazement that the House had permitted the presence among them of such men'. This, as Sir Wilfrid Lawson contended, undoubtedly was a reflection on the House, but the Speaker ignored this contention, and Sir Wilfrid did not pursue the matter further.

containing passages reflecting on the conduct of members of the House was referred to the Committee of Privileges. The article asserted that (1) private and confidential information as to what took place at private meetings of the Parliamentary Labour Party was conveyed by members of Parliament present at such meetings to newspapers; (2) one way in which such information was obtained was in return for a consideration paid by newspapers. Such consideration might be a retaining fee, payment for what was produced by the member in each particular case, or by personal publicity; (3) another way in which newspapers obtained such information was from members who were under the influence of drink; in order to obtain information in this way, newspapers' representatives offered intoxicants to members and paid for them and members accepted.

In their report the Committee of Privileges stated that the state of affairs which the article described was, if it in fact existed, one which would have at the least involved grave discredit to the members of the House. They therefore felt that they must inquire further as to what was the real truth of the matter, and they accordingly called before them a number of editors, journalists and others representing various newspapers which had published accounts of a private meeting of the Parliamentary Labour Party held on 23 April, that is to say, after the matter had been raised in the House. The Committee came to the conclusion that whilst in two cases there had been a departure from the high standard of personal honour which was to be expected from all members of Parliament, there was no evidence whatever to justify the general charges made in the article, and that these charges were wholly unfounded and constituted a grave contempt.

The grounds on which the Committee based their finding that these allegations constituted a grave contempt are stated in paragraphs 16 to 18 of their report, as follows:

> 16 . . . it has long been recognised that the publication of imputations reflecting on the dignity of the House or of any Member in his capacity as such is punishable as a contempt of Parliament. It is true that the imputation upon a member to come within this principle must relate

to something which he has done as such, that is to say, incidentally to and as part of his service to Parliament. . . . Reflections upon members, however, even where individuals are not named, may be so framed as to bring into disrepute the body to which they belong, and such reflections have therefore been treated as equivalent to reflections on the House itself. . . .

17. In modern times the practice of holding private meetings in the precincts of the Palace of Westminster of different parties has become well established and, in the view of Your Committee, it must be now taken to form a normal and everyday incident of Parliamentary procedure, without which the business of Parliament could not conveniently be conducted. Thus, meetings held within the precincts of the Palace of Westminster during the Parliamentary session are normally attended only by members as such, and the information which is given at such meetings is, in Your Committee's view, given to those attending them in their capacity as members. Your Committee therefore conclude on this matter that attendance of members at a private party meeting held in the precincts of the Palace of Westminster during the Parliamentary session, to discuss Parliamentary matters connected with the current or future proceedings of Parliament, is attendance in their capacity of Members of Parliament. It does not of course follow that this conclusion attracts to such meetings all the privileges which are attached to the transactions of Parliament as a whole.

18. It follows that an unfounded imputation in regard to such meetings involves an affront to the House as such. Your Committee consider that an unjustified allegation that Members regularly betray the confidence of private party meetings either for payment or whilst their discretion has been undermined by drink is a serious contempt.

To say that 'it has long been recognised that the publication of imputations reflecting on the dignity of the House or of any Member in his capacity as such is punishable as a contempt of Parliament' puts the case on the wrong footing. The statement implies that it is because reflections on the House are regarded as indignities to the House and reflections on members in their capacity as members as indignities to such members that such reflections are treated as contempts of Parliament. It is not for these reasons, but because reflections upon the character or proceedings of the House and reflections upon the character or conduct of members in their capacity as members tend to obstruct the House in the performance of its functions and members in the discharge of their duties that they are treated as contempts of Parliament or breaches of privilege.

More important, the law of Parliament applicable to the case is misstated. The statement that 'the imputation upon a member, to come within this principle', i.e. to constitute a contempt of Parliament, 'must refer to something which he has done as such [member], that is to say, incidentally to and part of his service to (*sic*) Parliament'* is incorrect. The rule is that to constitute a breach of privilege a libel upon a member must concern the character or conduct of the member in that capacity and the conduct or language on which the libel is based must be actions performed or words uttered in the actual transaction of the business of the House. Things not said or done by a member in the actual transaction of the business of the House might nevertheless be said to be done incidentally to and as part of his service in Parliament.

The statement that 'reflections upon members even when individuals are not named, may be so framed as to bring into disrepute the body to which they belong, and such reflections have therefore been treated as equivalent to reflections upon the House itself' is a quotation from a memorandum submitted to the Committee by Sir Gilbert (afterwards Lord) Campion, the Clerk of the House. Sir Gilbert did not support this statement by reference to any authority. It is, moreover, in complete antagonism with the statement in the fourteenth edition of May's *Parliamentary Practice* that 'reflections upon members, the particular individuals not being named or otherwise indicated, are equivalent to reflections on the House'. It may be doubted whether any imputation directed against members, however dishonourable the conduct imputed to them was, would bring the House into disrepute unless the members were unidentifiable. However this may be, it might be inferred from this state-

* Service *in* Parliament is the correct phrase.

ment that the rule as to the conditions which a reflection upon the character or conduct of members must fulfil if it is to be treated as a breach of privilege does not apply to reflections so framed as to bring the House into disrepute. Indeed, unless this inference is intended to be drawn, it is difficult to see what bearing the statement had on the question whether the allegation was a contempt of Parliament.

If, however, a reflection upon the conduct of members which did not relate to anything said or done by them in the House or a committee of the House could be treated as a contempt on the ground that it was framed in such a manner as to bring the House into disrepute, it would go a long way towards nullifying the rule in question. Indeed, it is difficult to see where the line could be drawn because the House could be brought into disrepute even by aspersions upon the conduct of members in private life, e.g. by an allegation that three-fourths of the members of the House of Commons were notorious evil-livers.

Even if it is admitted for the sake of argument that 'the practice of holding private meetings in the precincts of the Palace of Westminster [of members] of different parties must now be taken to form a normal and everyday incident of parliamentary procedure without which the business of Parliament could not conveniently be conducted', such meetings are not part of the proceedings of the House. It follows that an allegation that members regularly betrayed the confidence of private party meetings either for payment or whilst their discretion had been undermined by drink could not be said to be based upon matters arising in the actual transaction of the business of the House, and therefore could not constitute a contempt.

When the report of the Committee of Privileges was considered by the House, no motion 'that the House do agree with the Committee in their report' was moved. Instead the House resolved that the article in its general tone, and particularly by its unfounded imputations against unnamed members of insobriety in the precincts of the House, was an affront to the House, and that the writer of the article and the editor of the newspaper in which the article had appeared were guilty of contempt.

Although the conclusions of the Committee of Privileges

were thus rejected by implication, an inroad was nevertheless made on the accepted rule that in order to constitute a breach of privilege a libel upon a member must concern the character or conduct of the member in that capacity, and the conduct or language on which the libel is based must be actions performed or words uttered in the actual transaction of the business of the House. The imputation to unnamed members of insobriety within the precincts of the House undoubtedly tended to bring the House into disrepute, but it was not such a reflection on their conduct as would constitute a breach of privilege within the meaning of the rule. Nor could it be regarded as equivalent to a reflection on the House itself unless this rule is held not to apply to reflections on the conduct of members which are framed in such a way as to bring the body to which they belong into disrepute. The case may therefore be regarded as an authority in support of the contention that the rule in question does not apply to such reflections.

In a memorandum which he submitted to the Committee of Privileges in 1948 Sir Gilbert Campion, then Clerk of the House of Commons, said that 'to charge members individually or generally with extra-parliamentary conduct which renders them unworthy to sit in parliament may also in extreme circumstances be a libel on the House'. He did not cite any authority in support of this proposition, which was irreconcilable with the statement in the fourteenth edition of May's *Parliamentary Practice*, which he had edited, that 'aspersions upon the conduct of members . . . otherwise than in relation to parliament are not fit subjects for complaints to the House of Commons even if the inference is to be drawn that they are unworthy to sit in parliament'. The authority cited for this proposition was the statement by Mr Speaker Gully in 1896:

> In order to establish a case [of privilege] there must be some attack upon a member in respect of his conduct as a member of the House. In the present instance there is a violent attack, no doubt, on the character of the honourable member in respect of transactions outside the House altogether and therefore I do not think that it can constitute a case of [breach of] privilege, nor do I think the fact that the writer of the article draws or states an

> inference that if the charges are true then the honourable member against whom they are directed would not be fit to sit in the House – I do not think that that inference, merely at the end of an attack upon the honourable member in respect of matters outside the House would make that a breach of privilege what would not otherwise be so.

Possibly Sir Gilbert had in mind the motion made by Sir William Harcourt on 11 February 1890, 'that the publication in *The Times* newspaper of April 18, 1887, of a letter falsely alleged to be written by Mr. Parnell, and the comments thereupon in the said newspaper is a false and scandalous libel and a breach of the privileges of the House'. This letter had been published on the morning of the day on which the second reading of the Crimes Bill was to be taken. *The Times* expressed no doubt as to the authenticity of the letter, and confidently alleged that it was addressed to Patrick Egan, a notorious dynamiter. Its plain meaning was that Parnell had expressed sympathy with the Phoenix Park murders. Parnell denounced the letter as a forgery, but as the allegation did not relate to his parliamentary conduct the Speaker would not allow it to be raised as a breach of privilege. In 1888, however, a special commission consisting of three judges was appointed by Act of Parliament to inquire into the truth of charges and allegations made in *O'Donnell* v. *Walter*. This commission found that the letter was a forgery.

It is clear that the ground on which it was contended that the publication of the forged letter was a breach of privilege was not that it reflected upon Parnell's conduct, but the fact that, as Harcourt put it, the publication had been intended to affect the conduct and pervert the judgment of the House. If the motion had been carried the application of this principle could not have been confined to false imputations upon the extraparliamentary conduct of members; it would have been equally applicable to false statements of every description intended to influence the action of the House. An amendment declaring that the House declined to treat the publication in *The Times* newspaper of 18 April 1887 of a forged letter purporting to have been written by Mr Parnell and of the comments thereon as a breach of privilege of the House was carried to Harcourt's motion. Harcourt's contention had been anticipated by Sir Samuel Romilly eighty years before. In his *Memoirs*[4] he says that though he 'denied the power of the House to punish the publication of animadversions on the proceedings of the House or on the conduct of its members in matters which were concluded', he 'did not dispute the right of the House to imprison in all cases of breach of privilege which obstruct its proceedings, such as . . . publications on proceedings with a view to influence votes'.

In the memorandum referred to above Sir Gilbert Campion also stated that reflections on members in their capacity as members had in certain circumstances been ruled not to constitute a breach of privilege because *mala fides* was not imputed. The case he cited in support of this proposition does not bear it out. All that the Speaker said was that the publication complained of was 'not even a *prima facie* case of privilege'. Possibly Sir Gilbert confused this case with one in 1893 when complaint was made of an article in *The Times* alleging that one-half of the Irish Parliamentary Party were 'in receipt of a stipend drawn either from an English party fund or from the private liberality of rich English partisans', and describing the members in question as 'paid mercenaries'. The Speaker said that discourteous though the words might be, no *mala fides* was imputed to a member in the discharge of his duties in the House and he could not say a question of privilege was raised. The member who had brought the matter to the notice of the House 'respectfully submitted' that the decision whether a breach of privilege had been committed rested ultimately with the House, and, after the passage complained of had been read out by the Clerk at the Table, Gladstone pointed out that the article 'contained a most distinct charge of corruption – a charge of the reintroduction of corruption into the House after it had been happily clear from it during one hundred years, through the medium of the Irish members', and the Speaker said he must leave the matter in the hands of the House, which resolved that the passages complained of constituted a gross breach of privilege.

The House of Commons makes no distinction between defamatory speeches and defamatory writings. Indeed, passages in speeches which are the subject of complaint are often declared to be libels.

Complaints of breach of privilege should not be regarded as 'alternatives to actions for defamation'. The two proceedings are *diverso intuitu*. The object of an action for defamation is to secure for the plaintiff compensation for the wrongful loss of the esteem in which other people previously held him. The object of proceedings for contempt of the House by defaming one or more of its members, on the other hand, is to prevent or punish the obstruction of such member or members in the discharge of his or their duties. It is for this reason that the right to complain of such breaches of privileges is not restricted to the member or members against whose conduct the imputations are directed.

'The falsity of the libel is not an essential element in the offence.'[5] This may surprise those who approach the subject from the standpoint of the law of tort and forget that contempt of Parliament, like its analogue contempt of court, is a quasi-criminal offence and that, as Sir William Holdsworth has said, if defamation is regarded as a crime, 'truth as a defence is wholly out of place'.[6] On 25 October 1926 a complaint was made to the House of a speech made by a member and reported in a newspaper, in the course of which he had said he had seen many members drunk in the House of Commons and he was sorry to say no party was exempt. The member said he was not prepared to withdraw, modify or apologize for what he had said, and that if the House appointed a select committee or referred the matter to the Committee of Privileges, he was prepared to substantiate his allegations. The House rejected a proposal that the matter should be referred to the Committee of Privileges, and resolved that the speech was a gross libel on the members of the House and a grave breach of its privileges.

Reflections by members upon fellow members – above all, reflections upon the conduct of the Speaker – are regarded as graver offences than similar reflections by other persons. Thus in 1888 Mr Conybeare, a member, who wrote a letter to a newspaper saying that the acceptance by the Speaker of a motion to close the debate on the second reading of a local Bill introduced by the government after he (Mr Conybeare) had spoken for only a quarter of an hour was nothing short of a public scandal, was suspended from the service of the House for the remainder of the session or for one calendar month, whichever should first terminate. No action was, however, taken against the editor of the newspaper either for publishing the letter or for publishing an article commenting on the letter and stating that the Speaker was unfit for his position and that the sooner he was replaced by Mr Courtney, the Chairman of Ways and Means, the better for the dignity, the self-respect and the good order of the House of Commons.

The reason why reflections by members outside the House upon the conduct of the Speaker are regarded as particularly grave offences was thus stated by Gladstone in 1879, in the course of the discussion of a report in *The Times* of a speech by Parnell to which the attention of the House had been drawn. Parnell was reported to have said that 'if he were to tell them that the Speaker looked upon the Home Rule members much as a trapper would look upon vermin, he would in all probability incur his displeasure and the consequences of that displeasure'. Parnell denied that he had been making a speech. He had, he said, been giving a lecture on parliamentary procedure and had given the words complained of as an illustration of the kind of remark that would constitute a breach of privilege.

Gladstone said:

If any member of this House is so ill-advised on any occasion as to utter disparaging remarks outside the walls of this House in regard to the House itself, the House is so strong that . . . it can afford very well . . . to pass by remarks of that description. But there is one thing we neither can afford to do, nor ought we to desire to afford to do, and that is to tolerate any attack, direct or indirect, on the conduct of our Speaker. . . . His conduct is liable to be challenged in the House; and if it is challenged anywhere it ought to be challenged in the House. . . . The very best Speaker that sat in that chair – and, happily, it is hardly necessary to draw a comparison between one Speaker and another – cannot possibly be known outside the House as he is known within it; and therefore any assault or attack upon the Speaker outside the House never can carry with it its own cure, while an attack within the House ought to carry its own cure.

Examples of imputations against the conduct of members which have in recent years been held to constitute breaches of privilege are imputations of partiality and other misconduct in the chair directed against the Speaker, the Chairman of Ways and Means, and the chairman of a standing committee, imputations of partiality and unfairness on the part of the members of committees on opposed private Bills or other select committees discharging quasi-judicial duties, imputations of improper motives in the discharge of their parliamentary duties, e.g. imputing to members that they were opposing a Bill for financial reasons and allegations against members of drunkenness in the House.

In 1887 the House 'declined to treat' the publication of an article in *The Times* charging John Dillon, a leading member of the Irish Party, with deliberate and intentional untruth in a speech made in the House as a breach of privilege. According to Lord George Hamilton, the member who drew the attention of the House to the article and moved that the publication of the article was a breach of privilege, did so under the mistaken impression that if the motion was carried, the editor of *The Times* would be ordered to attend the House and, on his appearance at the bar, would be able to produce his proofs of this and other statements in the article. After a desultory debate of an hour or two, the debate was adjourned. When it was resumed, Sir Edward Clarke, the Solicitor-General, was put up to move an amendment declaring that the House 'declined to treat' the publication of the article as a breach of privilege. In his *Autobiography*, Clarke says that together with Sir Richard Webster, the Attorney-General, afterwards Lord Alverstone, Lord Chief Justice, he 'advised the government that the article did not constitute a breach of privilege', and that he 'was commissioned to propose an amendment in that sense', but that when Lord Randolph Churchill, whom ministers 'were nervously anxious not to offend', was shown the terms of the amendment, he said 'he would not support it in that form, so it was altered at the very moment that I rose to speak into a statement that the House declines to treat it as a breach of privilege'.

The words 'declines to treat as a breach of privilege' were ambiguous. They did not, in terms, assert that a breach of privilege had not been committed, as Goschen, who spoke last for the government, pointed out. Indeed, Lord Randolph Churchill, while supporting the amendment, said 'with much frankness and candour' that, 'from a technical point of view, no sane or reasonable person could entertain the slightest doubt that there had been a breach of the privileges of the House of Commons'. On the other hand, it was unlikely that many people outside the House would appreciate the subtle difference between declining to treat the charge as a breach of privilege and denying that it was one. Indeed it was more than likely that they would regard it as implying that the charge was true. Moreover, Clarke, who had come down prepared to contend that the publication of the article did not constitute a breach of privilege, did not change his line of argument. He said that he had not found, and did not believe anyone could find, an instance of the House of Commons committing to prison a person for an accusation made by him against a member which was not an accusation of corruption or of misfeasance in a vote given in the House or an attempt to coerce or intimidate him in his action in the House. Sir Charles Russell, afterwards Lord Russell of Killowen, Lord Chief Justice, replied that there was no justification in any textbook or in the works of any writer on constitutional law that he was aware of for the distinction Clarke sought to draw between the different kinds of imputations of misconduct upon members, some of which would, and some would not, be breaches of privilege. It is, indeed, difficult to see how anyone whose judgment was not perverted by party prejudice could have doubted that the publication of the allegation was a breach of privilege. As Gladstone said, 'if there be such a thing as a breach of privilege at all, surely a charge [against a member] of wilful and deliberate falsehood committed in the discharge of parliamentary duties, constitutes a breach of privilege'. The amendment was carried by a party vote.

All doubts on the question whether such an allegation would constitute a breach of privilege have now been removed. On 20 June 1963 the House of Commons resolved, *nem. con.*, that a member, who had since ceased to be a member of the House, in making a personal statement to the House on 22 March 1963, which he later admitted not to be true, was guilty of a gross contempt of the House. To charge a member with having done what, if done, would constitute a gross contempt of the House, must itself be a contempt.

The last case with which it is proposed to deal is one which is of interest not because of its subject matter, but because of what the Committee of Privileges said in their report. On 24 March 1964 a complaint concerning the following passage in a speech made by Mr Quintin Hogg, a member, was referred to the Committee of Privileges:

> No honest person since we came into power can accuse us of pursuing a reactionary or illiberal policy. Nevertheless, our elbows have been jarred in almost every part of the world by individual Labour members' partisanship of subversive activities. This is the party which is now seeking power.

In paragraph 4 of their report the Committee stated that the question which had to be decided was 'whether (a) there [had] been a contempt of the House in the sense that disgrace or ignominy had been cast upon it as an institution or (b) it [had] been brought into disgrace'. It would appear from paragraph 5 that the Committee deduced this from what they said was 'an established principle', viz. that reflections upon members, whether the particular individuals were indicated or not, could in some circumstances be equivalent to reflections on the House itself' (paragraph 5). There is, in fact, no such 'established principle'. The Committee must have misunderstood, at any rate they misquoted, the statement in May's *Parliamentary Practice* which they cited in support of theirs, viz. the statement that 'reflections upon members, the particular individuals not being named or otherwise indicated, *are* equivalent to reflections on the House itself'. As has already been explained, this statement goes too far. But even if it had been an established principle that reflections upon members, whether the particular individuals were indicated or not, could in some circumstances be equivalent to reflections on the House itself, it would not follow that no reflection upon members would constitute a breach of privilege unless it was equivalent to a reflection on the House itself.

The Committee concluded in the light of the considerations in paragraphs 5 to 8 of their report, and of the fuller explanation of his words and of their intended meaning given by Mr Hogg, that there had not been any contempt of the House. It is not altogether clear what these considerations were, but as Mr Selwyn Lloyd, who was the chairman of the Committee, subsequently said that 'the law and the practice' – by which he presumably meant that part of the law of Parliament which relates to contempt of Parliament and the practice of the House – were 'stated very clearly in paragraphs 7 and 8', they are set out below.

> 7. Your Committee recognise that it is the duty of the House to deal with such reflections upon members as tend, or may tend, to undermine public respect for and confidence in the House itself as an institution. But they think that when the effect of particular imputations is under consideration regard must be had to the importance of preserving freedom of speech in matters of political controversy and also, in cases of ambiguity, to the intention of the speaker. It seems to them particularly important that the law of parliamentary privilege should not, except in the clearest case, be invoked so as to inhibit or discourage the formation and free expression of opinion outside the House by members equally with other citizens in relation to the conduct of the affairs of the nation.
> 8. It has long been accepted that neither House of Parliament has any power to create new privileges. Your Committee believe that it would be contrary to the interest of the House and of the public to widen the interpretation of its privileges especially in matters affecting freedom of speech. Your Committee and the House are not concerned with setting standards for political comment or for the propriety, accuracy or taste of speeches made on public platforms outside parliament. They are concerned only with the protection of the reputation, the character and the good name of the House itself. It is in that respect

only and for that limited purpose that they are concerned with imputations against the conduct of individual members.

There is scarcely one sentence in either of these paragraphs that is not untrue or at least disputable. The statement in paragraph 7: 'Your Committee recognise that it is the duty of the House to deal with such reflections upon members as tend, or may tend, to undermine public respect for and confidence in the House itself as an institution', read in conjunction with the statements in paragraph 8: 'Your Committee and the House . . . are concerned only with the protection of the reputation, the character and the good name of the House itself. It is in that respect only and for that limited purpose that they are concerned with imputations against the conduct of individual members', implies that it is not the duty, and has not been the practice, of the House to deal with reflection upon individual members unless such reflections tend or may tend to undermine public respect for and confidence in the House itself. That the House in exercising its jurisdiction over contempts has been concerned only to protect its reputation, character and good name is simply not true. On the contrary the precedents show that the House has always considered that it was its duty to protect its members from obstruction in the discharge of their duties by scandalous or libellous imputations directed against them as well as by physical molestation.

Granted that it is important that freedom of speech in matters of political controversy should be preserved, it is difficult to see what bearing this consideration could have on the question whether a particular imputation against the conduct of a member tended or might tend to undermine public respect for, and confidence in, the House itself. This is a quasi-judicial decision into which considerations of prudence or expediency should not enter.

That when the effect of particular imputations against the conduct of members is under consideration regard must be had, in cases of ambiguity, to the intention of the speaker is a novel doctrine. The true test, as the Committee of Privileges observed in 1951, is not what was the intention of the speaker, but what effect the words he used would be reasonably likely to have upon those who heard them, and any who subsequently read a report of them.

It is not clear whether the admonition conveyed by the statement 'it is important that the law of parliamentary privilege' – by which the Committee doubtless meant the power of the House to punish breaches of privilege and other contempts – 'should not, except in the clearest case, be invoked so as to inhibit or discourage the formation and free expression of opinion outside the House . . . in relation to the conduct of the affairs of the nation' was addressed to the House or to M.P.s individually. Considering how temperately – the word is that of F. W. Maitland, the historian, not the writer's – the House has used this power during this and the preceding century, that assembly would not seem to stand in any need of such advice. If, on the other hand, the object of the Committee, was, as has been suggested, to deter members from bringing what they deem breaches of privilege to the notice of the House, this scarcely appears to have fallen within the limits of the inquiry entrusted to them. In any case it is no less important that freedom of speech outside the House should not be used so as to inhibit or discourage the free expression of opinion within it.

Enough, it is hoped, has been said to demonstrate that this report cannot be regarded as an authoritative exposition of the law of Parliament. Before leaving the subject, however, the writer cannot refrain from expressing his surprise that the Committee should have supposed that the House could, presumably by the use of its power of committing for contempt, widen the interpretation of its privileges. The House of Commons can no more widen the interpretation of any of its privileges than it can add to them. Indeed, to talk of widening the interpretation of the privilege of committing for contempt is meaningless, the privilege being, like its analogue the jurisdiction of committing for contempt of court, 'practically arbitrary and unlimited'.[7]

References

1 *Constitutional History* (2nd ed.), vol. 1, p. 443.
2 341 U.S. 367 at p. 377.
3 May, *Parliamentary Practice* (5th ed.), p. 93.

4 Vol. 2, pp. 308–9.
5 May, *Parliamentary Practice* (17th ed.), p. 138.
6 'Defamation in the 16th and 17th Centuries', *Law Quarterly Review*, Vol. 40, p. 305.
7 Per Jessel, M.R. in *Re Clements, Republic of Costa Rica* v. *Erlanger*, 46 L.J. Ch. 375, at p. 385.

Appendix I

My Day in Court

Harold Laski

On 16 June 1945 Professor Harold Laski, then Chairman of the Labour Party, went to Newark in Nottinghamshire to speak on behalf of the local candidate in the General Election. During questions, a member of the audience, Mr Wentworth Day, asked a question, an account of which was given in the *Newark Advertiser* a few days later. The account of the meeting said,

> Mr. Day asked the Professor why he had openly advocated 'revolution by violence' in speaking at Bishops Stortford and Bournemouth during the war. . . . Professor Laski replied that . . . if Labour did not obtain what it needed by general consent, 'we shall have to use violence even if it means revolution'. When people felt it was the moment for great experiment, for innovation, because when war is over people so easily forget – especially those who had the power in their hands – that was the time for experiment. Great changes were so urgent in this country, and if they were not made by consent they would be made by violence, and judging by the temper his questioner had displayed he would be perfectly naturally one of the objects of violence when it came.

Many other newspapers repeated the article.

Laski's version of his heckler's intervention and the reply he gave was that after the great upheaval of war the people of a country were conditioned to change. If change was not forthcoming the workers felt it was an intolerable burden. In that way a society drifted into violence. But since Britain had the power to achieve change by consent, we were not committed as other nations to achieving evolution by violence.

Laski was bound to start libel proceedings against the various newspapers, since his recorded remarks, if they went unchallenged, were reckoned to do incalculable harm to the Labour cause. Once he was committed by the issue of a writ, his pride and reputation were at stake so that the action could not decently be discontinued.

The case inevitably attracted wide publicity. Laski himself was a popular figure among his students at the London School of Economics, and his position in the Labour Party commanded respect. The trial was held in the Lord Chief Justice's Court before Lord Goddard and a City of London Special Jury. Mr G. O. (now Mr Justice) Slade, Q.C., an expert in libel law, appeared for Laski, and Sir Patrick Hastings, the leading advocate of his day, appeared for the *Daily Express*, the paper chosen to fight the test action.

It was the duel between Laski and Hastings that may have determined the action. Hastings, at his most subtle and incisive, made Laski look helpless and evasive. His first question was devastating (Hastings always made a point of selecting his first question carefully). He asked: 'Mr. Laski, do you believe that the use of violence to achieve your political ends is practically inevitable?' Laski could not supply an answer, yes or no. Even the 'no' had to be qualified, but Laski's insistence to qualify it at length gave the jury an immediate bad impression and allowed Hastings – perhaps unfairly – to cut him short with an additional question. 'Is the answer "No!" ', to which Laski, cut off in full flight of oratorical explanation, could say only 'The answer is "no" '.

The jury, after retiring for forty minutes, found that the report in the *Newark Advertiser* was a fair and accurate report of a public meeting. They spared Laski the humiliation of having to hear a possibly adverse verdict from the jury on the question whether his speeches and writings throughout his life advocated and incited his fellow countrymen to violence and revolution.

If hope is a stimulant beyond any other, nothing is quite so decisive as failure. You may be beaten in a game and enjoy, nevertheless, the pleasure of combat. You may be 'plucked' in an examination and yet know that it is a temporary setback you will overcome in a month. You may even be routed in a skirmish and rest confident in the knowledge that it is only part of a larger campaign. But when you are beaten in the courts of law there is a kind of dumb finality about it which I can only compare with the ultimate emphasis of death.

Every element in a civil trial goes to deepen this sense of finality. In the proceedings themselves you are almost bound to feel like a marionette. The speeches on both sides seem remote from the events you knew; they are like blood in a test tube compared with blood in a living person. You know, of course, that it is about you the lawyers are talking, but all that they say seems to have lost its colour, its vividness, its sense of life, and to be reduced to a shadowlike skeleton which will never be clothed once more in flesh and blood. You only seem a human being when you are in the witness box and counsel on the other side is speaking about you and cross-examining you.

As you listen to this speech and watch the mask-like faces in the jury box, you wonder if it is about yourself that he is talking. You remember the ardour of the incident, the enthusiasm of your effort – the devotion that sent you on a journey of hours for those seventy or eighty minutes of propaganda. Are you really that figure of evil, was your intent always so evil, did you always seem to those political opponents whom you sought to convince an enemy so bitter and so maleficent? Did the pages you wrote over so many years, in so eager an effort to persuade, to find a common mind in which your fellow citizens could share, really read to them all the while like the effort of an Iago pouring some subtle poison into the ears of your opponents? Did that crowd really think you a Cataline, weaving the web of some vile conspiracy, when you thought that what you were urging was the magnanimity that gives birth to conciliation?

The *persona* which the leader of your opponents makes with so much artifice from the complex alchemy of your character is well calculated to leave you certainly disturbed, and possibly almost stunned – but you must listen to it all with passive restraint. It is your enemies' hour, and they must enjoy it to the full. It is for the pleasure of this barrage that they have unmasked their batteries, probed all your motives, dissected with all the hostility they could muster ends and ideas that you do not even recognise as your own.

And you are then handed over to that same counsel whose life has so largely been passed in pricking men until they bleed. He performs his war-dance about you like a dervish intoxicated by the sheer ecstasy of his skill in his own performance, ardent in his knowledge that, if you trip for one second, his knife is at your throat. He makes a pattern from bits and pieces picked with care from a pattern of life you have been steadily weaving for a quarter of a century to prove either that you never meant what you intended, or that you lacked every element of skill to give the world the sense of your intent. He moves between the lines of sarcasm and insult. It is an effort to tear off, piece by piece, the skin which he declares no more than a mask behind which any man of understanding could have grasped the foulness of your purpose. He treats you, not as a human being, but as a surgeon might treat some specimen he is demonstrating to students in a dissecting room.

And, all the time, there sits above you the brooding and impassive judge, to whom this operation is no more than another day in an endless routine of similar days; while facing you are the seven impassive men and women to whom it is a kind of play in which they are half actors, half spectators. You know that no small part of your fate is in their hands; and not the least barbarous pain in this grim process is your tortured doubt of whether they have grasped even a small part of your effort to draw some thread of clarity through the vast web of organised confusion your executioner has sought to thrust upon them. You dare not answer too fully lest they be wearied; and you dare not answer too briefly lest they should misunderstand. And at every moment the fear shoots across your mind that every nuance of this embittered argument is, in fact, a passage in a play they have never seen before and judged quite worthless even before they were chosen – mostly against their will – to witness its staging.

For some time you cease to be the principal villain, and move, though always in the sight of the audience, to the wings of the stage. Then you must watch the effort of your enemies to break in pieces the confidence of the witnesses who have come to support your fate. Mostly, they are simple folk, honest, straightforward, unsubtle. Mostly, they have never been in the High Court before, let alone appeared there as witnesses. Counsel for the defendant is mainly concerned to throw them off their balance, to confuse them, to shrug them with a lift of his shoulders into people about whom he and the jury share a common and private contempt.

When the witnesses on both sides have been done with, you have to sit once more with Buddha-like impassivity while the counsel for your opponent sums up for his client. Here, at least he is simple and direct; he knows precisely the effect he desires to produce on the jury. He assures them that he will make the complex material that has been put before them so simple that their minds can be at ease and confident. He paints your character in a few incisive sentences. You begin to see the outlines of an evil enemy of the realm, clever enough to dress up his long-cherished stratagems in garments skilfully designed to conceal their nefarious purpose. You are in substance like a figure in one of those Elizabethan dramas which Machiavelli influenced; noble men have worked with you, innocent of the ugly ends for which you proposed to use their alliance. You hear attributed to yourself principles you have never held. You find yourself driven by motives you have never known yourself to possess. You become, indeed, the supreme and ardent enemy of the very cause you have sought to serve. But now, he concludes triumphantly, we have torn the mask off the villain; he can no longer disguise himself as an honourable servant of a great movement; he stands revealed before you as one who has striven all his life to undermine the foundations of social peace.

To yourself, listening to what seems the demented passion of a rhetoric devoid of any content save its appeal to the emotions of men and women ready to see in any proponent of social change the grim outline of a Marat or a Robespierre, your own counsel's final speech comes as a great relief. If you know his argument by heart, at least it is a profound psychological comfort to hear it marshalled with orderly effectiveness, and to see the vital points of substance given their due emphasis. You feel that the ease with which he pricks the rhetorical bubbles your opponent's counsel has so lustily blown cannot fail to impress itself upon any men and women with open minds. As he drives home a pattern of events in the shape in which it has become part of your own consciousness, you convince yourself, or almost, that the imperturbable figure on the Bench, trained to weigh evidence, skilled in the separation of fact from fiction, careful to eliminate from his own mind and, if he can, from the minds of the jury, all impact that prejudice may have sought to make – that now, at long last, truth will emerge unscathed from all effort to twist and contort it into shapes you do not recognise.

The judge seems a kindly old man, with a winning smile that lights up his eyes. He speaks with unemphatic quietness, so that, sometimes, you have even to bend forward to catch what he says to the jury in an easy, almost conversational tone. When he tells them of some point the defence has made, or, with a half-amused smile, describes to them the nature of a political campaign, or urges them to realise the passionate care the Bench has taken to safeguard the Englishman's right to the fullest freedom of discussion, you almost feel that you are back in some pleasant lecture room of an Oxford college where an elderly don is retailing the details of some ancient trial decided long ago.

Then, suddenly, his transition to another part of the evidence makes you wonder when he is going to stress that point in the first part which told so strongly in your favour; how he is going to comment on the curious methods of this witness, the subtle way in which your opponent's counsel tore endless passages from their context to paint his picture of your ugly purposes. He will not, surely, forget your counsel's comment on this suggestive point; he cannot have failed to notice that vital combination of circumstances so carefully omitted from the speech in which your opponent's counsel sought to prevent the jury from seeing the gap it revealed in his case. You cannot believe that he will studiously refrain from noting that the charges made against all you have ever said or written these twenty years not only have never been made before, but, were they true, ought obviously to have resulted in your appearance in the dock at Old Bailey. At some time, you are confident, he will bid the jury take notice of the massive testimony your own witnesses have given without an effort at serious contradiction. At least, so you think in growing uneasiness, he will remember that in your five-hour duel with opposing counsel.

you stood your ground, answered with straightforward clarity, did not fall into the traps he laid that you might grow angry or confused or irritated, and so be led into the situation where he is so notoriously able to have a witness at his mercy.

And then, with a sudden gasp, you realise that he is not going to put your case at all. He makes his point; he is careful always to emphasise to the attentive jury that it is for them, and them only, to choose whether they will accept the points he makes. But they are always your opponent's points, and you note, almost within the first half-hour of his summing up, that he is conveying, not without some subtlety, what Mr Justice Holmes meant when he said that judicial decisions depend upon the 'inarticulate major premises' of the man on the Bench. And you understand at that stage that the case is lost.

The judge not only hates the opinions you hold, but will explain to the jury that they are dangerous opinions. And since, at your opponent's instance, the jury is a 'special' jury, you know how unlikely it is that they will have an atom of concern for anyone with dangerous opinions. What, you swiftly see, is the real issue at stake is not what was said at some place on a definite occasion, but the fact that you hold unpopular opinions which both judge and jury are convinced it is bad to hold and worse by far to express.

That is the moment when you cease to be an actor in the legal drama, and become one more among the packed spectators in the Court. You know the result of your case. Everything that follows is as regular and automatic as winding up a clock. What had enshrouded you in its air of legal majesty is now like a play upon the stage of which you had read the end before ever you entered the theatre. The actors continue their parts, for the play must be officially closed. But you are already planning what you will say by way of thanks and consolation to your solicitors and counsel, who had worked so hard and been, to your mind, both fair and effective. You are wondering whether there is a back way out of the Court, that you may avoid the relentless stare of the crowds at the door, the inexorable click of the cameramen from the different papers thrust into your face, the comments on the result you are likely to hear if you go home by bus or tube. You pray that some car may be at hand in which you may be hidden from that restless anxiety of the stream of journalists who, with notebooks ready poised, sweep down upon you, like vultures upon a corpse, to seize your private thoughts for a public avid for any sensation even if it take but three lines to express.

There is no safety for you until you sit at your own fireside. There, at least, without the stare of a thousand eyes, you can meditate upon the shades of meaning in the historic phrase 'the equal protection of the laws'. At least you have been given the fulfilment of the Englishman's right to seek his remedy for injustice and have his day in court.

Appendix II

Punitive Damages and the PQ 17 Libel Case*

'Justinian'

We are all creatures of habit. It is not surprising, therefore, that a device which we employ in our daily lives should find itself embedded in the law. The broad use of precedent, in the sense of the employment of past decisions as guide for the making of future decisions, is a feature of every legal system. The English lawyer, in a laudable desire to attain certainty in the law, has evolved the doctrine of binding precedent, whereby lower courts are bound to (not just may) follow the reasoning adopted in higher courts' decision.

Imagine, then, the astonishment of the legal profession when the Court of Appeal deliberately declined recently to follow faithfully a clear ruling of the House of Lords in 1964. The case was *Broome* v. *Cassell & Co. Ltd and Irving* (the PQ 17 libel case). The action was for a libel on Captain John Egerton Broome, R.N. (retired), the escort commander of the ill-fated convoy, PQ 17, to the Soviet Union, which in 1942 was severely mauled by German submarines after the scattered convoy had lost its naval protection.

Great detail

David Irving, the author, and Cassells, the publishers, produced an 'historical' account of the incident that put the blame on Captain Broome. Every other commentator or naval historian had exonerated Captain Broome. In essence, Captain Broome alleged that Mr Irving in his book had laid at his door the responsibility for shameful conduct by the Royal Navy.

* From *Financial Times* 15 March 1971.

Captain Broome further pointed to passages in the book which he said imputed to him 'downright disobedience' and 'cowardly desertion of the convoy'.

The trial jury awarded Captain Broome damages of £15,000 by way of compensation for loss of reputation and another £25,000 as punitive damages for the outrageous and shocking conduct of both author and publishers. The appeal to the Court of Appeal focused on the element of punitive damages. Author and publishers contended that such head of damage was awardable in only very limited circumstances, explained in great detail by the House of Lords, that did not fit the facts of the PQ 17 case.

The legal argument on the place of punitive damages awarded for libel and the basis for calculating any such award was seemingly coloured by the judges' views of the conduct of the author. Lord Justice Phillimore observed that Mr Irving's book was 'anti-British and a deliberate attack on the Royal Navy.' Lord Denning said that 'the condemnation was made twenty years later by Mr Irving who was a small boy at the time'. But no one doubted that Mr Irving had thoroughly researched the subject matter of his book. What then did it matter that he was hardly out of his cradle when the PQ 17 convoy met its fate? His non-involvement in the events of those years may have given him an initial detachment so as to sustain a degree of objectivity, even if, as the judges found, he finally jettisoned the strict code of scholarship.

Doubtless the facts of the libel action inclined their Lordships to uphold the power of the courts to punish authors who transgress the rules of good manners. What has astounded members of the legal profession has been the sight of the Court of Appeal wriggling free of the binding precedent of a House of Lords decision.

Libel damages traditionally fall into three categories. 'Compensatory' damages represent in money the amount of a defamed person's damage to his reputation. It includes any quantifiable financial loss suffered as a result of the libel. Then there are 'aggravated' damages which are in fact a branch of compensatory damages. They seek to compensate for injury to the feelings of the injured party where the author has made the defamation peculiarly offensive. It was the third category, 'punitive' damages, that was in issue.

The place of punitive damages in the civil law was authoritatively dealt with by the House of Lords in the famous trade union case in 1964, *Rookes* v. *Barnard*. Lord Devlin, in a masterly and illuminating judgment to which all his four brethren unqualifiedly subscribed, re-examined the whole area of punitive damages and restated the law of England in modern, socially acceptable terms. He declared that high-handed, malicious, insolent or arrogant conduct, which involved the commission of an actionable wrong, would not found an award of punitive damages, but he did not abolish them. His inclination to extirpate punitive damages was based on two considerations.

Victim's loss

To allow a court to punish a wrongdoer beyond the bounds of compensation to his victim would be to confuse the functions of the civil and the criminal law. Damages should take into account all the features of the victim's loss without imposing any further penalty on the wrongdoer. Lord Devlin did not discuss fully whether if punishment and deterrence were legitimate objects of the civil law, they did in fact have that effect. Criminologists generally reject the deterrent value of punishment in the criminal law, mainly on the ground that deterrence is unprovable in fact. One might add that to demonstrate statistically the efficacy of punitive damages as a deterrent may be as impossible as to demonstrate statistically the efficacy of prayer. Hence, we might as well abandon legal policies founded on the assumption of their deterrent value.

Lord Devlin, however, stopped short of the logical conclusion of his argument. He retained punitive damages in three limited circumstances: (a) Where there is oppressive, arbitrary or unconstitutional action by Government servants; (b) where the wrongdoer's conduct has been calculated by him to make a profit which might well exceed compensation payable to his victim; and (c) where such damages are expressly authorized by statute. This exegesis on the law of damages deliberately threw over the common law position that punitive damages were awardable in any cases where the court thought that the defamer ought to be further punished over and above the payment of compulsory damages.

All or nothing

Lord Devlin's formula for the future may be criticized, not least on the ground that it was incongruous of the House of Lords to declare its freedom from being bound by its own previous decisions and then suggesting that it would be impious and disrespectful if the Law Lords were to ignore totally their own precedents. The argument over punitive damages is an all-or-nothing situation. Either punitive damages should be available, or they have no part to play in the civil law.

But one thing was manifest. For all the lower courts the law of England, after 1964, was as stated by the House of Lords in the form of Lord Devlin's speech. However much the Court of Appeal thought (even justifiably) that Lord Devlin's reasoning was defective, it was its duty to abide by the law and give effect to it. Nothing daunted, Lord Denning and his colleagues said that Lord Devlin 'must have overlooked or misunderstood' the earlier decisions of the House of Lords, and they invoked the Latin tag *per incuriam* (by mistake) to avoid having to follow the Lords. Instead the Court of Appeal reverted to the law as it was pre-1964.

The Court of Appeal was not only audacious in the face of a well established rule of precedent. But it also, by a judicial somersault, threw the law of damages into confusion. Whose statement of the law does a trial judge now adopt in directing himself or a jury? This is to say nothing of the doctrine of precedent which is in disarray.